Exceptional Speaking

Exceptional Speaking

THE LEADER'S PLAYBOOK FOR WORLD CLASS PERSUASIVE PRESENTATIONS

Jane Anderson

Editing: Kristen Lowrey

Typeset by BookPOD

ISBN: 978-0-6485022-6-5 (pbk)
eISBN: 978-0-6485022-7-2 (ebook)

NATIONAL
LIBRARY
OF AUSTRALIA

A catalogue record for this
book is available from the
National Library of Australia

Writing *Exceptional Speaking* has been a journey of growth, learning and collaboration over the last 14 years, and I'm still learning the art and science of speaking every day. This book would not have been possible without the guidance, support and inspiration of so many incredible individuals.

First, I want to express my deepest gratitude to my clients and community of thought leaders. Your commitment to excellence, your courage to step into the spotlight, and your trust in my guidance have been the driving force behind this book. You inspire me every day to continue my mission of empowering female leaders to thrive with confidence and clarity.

To my family, your unwavering support and belief in me have been my foundation. To my husband, Mark, thank you for your patience and encouragement, for laughing at my jokes and telling me the ones that needed work.

A heartfelt thank you goes to my editor, Kristen Lowrey, who brought structure and polish to my thoughts while keeping the essence of my voice intact. Your expertise and attention to detail have elevated this book to new heights.

To Sylvie Blair at Bookpod, thank you for your hard work in bringing this vision to life. From the design to the distribution, your professionalism and commitment have made this book possible.

To my mentors and peers, Matt Church, Keith Abraham, Neil McCallum, Gabrielle Dolan, Robbie Mack, Troy and Zara Love, Jennifer Leone, Kate Burr, Emma McQueen, Corrinne Armour and Dr Louise Mahler, your wisdom and candid feedback have challenged me to refine my ideas and strengthen my message. You've shaped not only this book but also the growth of my career, and I am forever grateful for your influence.

A special thank you to my readers—whether this is your first step into the world of public speaking or you're honing your craft, your dedication to personal growth is what makes this work so rewarding. I am honoured to be part of your journey and hope that *Exceptional Speaking* serves as a resource you return to time and again.

Lastly, to every woman who has ever doubted her voice, know this: your story, your expertise, and your message have the power to transform lives. I wrote this book for you—to inspire you to stand tall, speak boldly, and share your brilliance with the world.

With gratitude and admiration,

Jane

CONTENTS

INTRODUCTION

> *'All the great speakers were*
> *bad speakers at first.'*
> — Ralph Waldo Emerson

People often compliment me on my ability to present – to give keynotes and speeches and even deliver workshops well.

They'll say, 'You're just an incredible speaker.' 'You're such a natural!' And, 'It must come so easily to you.'

The thing is that I'm not – and it doesn't.

The honest fact is that I'm not a natural speaker. And I don't have an innate talent for presenting. I'm certainly not writing this book because I'm talented or natural or because speaking comes easily to me (because it absolutely doesn't). I'm writing this book because if I can become a world-class speaker garnering world-class fees, who is asked to deliver to thousands both in Australia and overseas, then so can you – in fact, so can anyone!

Glenn Capelli is a professional speaker and author who delivers hugely impactful presentations each and every time he takes the stage. He says that when it comes to speaking, 'you want to get good and then you want to get known.' He's absolutely right.

When you're just beginning your speaking journey, it's good to be low on the totem pole, to be delivering to smaller crowds and receiving a smaller fee (or maybe even no fee). This gives you the opportunity to hone your craft (and speaking is, without a doubt, a craft) and learn the skills needed both to deliver and to prepare to deliver. And you can do it all before you are standing on a stage in front of 1000 people.

And let me tell you, you certainly don't want to be doing it while you're on stage in front of 1000 people!

Why do I know that? Because that's exactly what happened to me.

When I first began my speaking journey, the subject of personal branding was hugely popular. Everyone wanted speakers that could cover this topic and I was one of the few at the time with this area of expertise. So rather than getting good before I got known, I got known before I got good. And I felt like I was flying the plane straight off the cliff.

The fact that I was booking bigger venues and more expensive gigs before I really felt like I had my feet under me caused me a huge amount of anxiety. I was often in the panic zone, scrambling to learn the skills of speaking and running a speaker business while actually doing the speaking. I would talk to other speakers that I admired and ask them things like, 'How do you structure your keynotes?' 'What do you say first... or second?' 'How do you remember everything?' 'How do you manage the process?' 'When do you follow up? And how?'

But many of these speakers were just so intuitive that they couldn't really share a 'structure' per se. Or they weren't sure how to put into words the things that worked for them. And to be honest, many didn't understand the business either.

So, I'd sit in the audience, listening to these amazing speakers, and trying to map out the structure of their keynotes. How they presented the theme (and when), how many main points they'd make, and how many sub-points, as well as any other ideas I could glean.

It was not a good way to go about it, and even though I was learning, I had a lot of disasters because I was still flying by the seat of my pants. I didn't have the skills that I needed to present, I didn't have the structure that allowed me to convey my message and I didn't have the business knowledge to run a speaking business well. In fact, it wasn't until I worked with one of the top 10 keynote speakers in the world, Matt Church, that I finally had a structure template to draw from. From there I started to develop the skills that I really needed to speak and speak well. And then I was able to build my speaking business too.

My early failures are not my favourite memories, but it's important I share them because the successes that I have had as a speaker were not due to natural talent or innate skills. Instead, my successes came down to hard work, working out how to overcome anxiety, spending time learning speaking skills – such as how to structure a keynote – figuring out how to really commercialise my speaking, and, finally, practise, practise, practise. It didn't happen overnight, but it did happen. I've since gone on to coach other speakers and leaders in organisations and the message I want you to take away from this book is that if I can do it, you can do it. You really can.

This book is designed to introduce you to the main elements that will help you take your speaking practice to the next level – to exceptional speaking. I want you to see and believe that you can be world-class, command global stages with the highest fees and commercialise your time on the stage even if you also aren't a naturally talented or intuitive speaker. By applying the things in this book, you can get there!

And if you have any questions, be sure to reach out. I'd love to help!

CHAPTER 1

WHY EXCEPTIONAL SPEAKING MATTERS

'The worst speech you'll ever give will be far better than the one you never give.'
— **Fred Miller**

When I first started speaking, I was scared to death. I'd been a trainer for 15 years and I was used to being in front of audiences. But while I was used to training, the whole speaking thing was a different story.

I vividly remember the first keynote I ever gave at an event. There were 70 people in attendance and as I stood on stage, I found myself suddenly reverting to facilitating mode. I felt like all eyes were on me, and I was more concerned about what people were doing and thinking than what I was saying.

"

People often
ask me how I get
over my nerves prior
to speaking in public. I
always have a bit of a
laugh because really,
I never do.

"

Instead of delivering a well thought out presentation, I fell back to my training and facilitation roots and began asking questions. I realised I was turning a keynote into a training session and could see that wasn't the right way to deliver. I was completely taken aback by this response and I suddenly felt so inadequate. This was the moment I realised that training was not speaking, but I also didn't know what to do differently.

I could have let my first speaking experience throw me off ever speaking again. And after that event I did vow to never, ever be in that situation again. But rather than quitting completely, I decided to arm myself with knowledge. So I began speaker training. This was a vital part of helping me to turn my experience around.

Our fear of public speaking

Jerry Seinfeld said, *'According to most studies, people's number one fear is public speaking. Number two is death. Death is number two. Does that sound right? This means to the average person, if you go to a funeral, you're better off in the casket than doing the eulogy.'*

I'm not sure how true that is, but being fearful of public speaking is extremely common. Nerves, emotions and insecurities certainly don't discriminate and can impact even the most confident people. It may feel like there are people who are naturally gifted at public speaking and others who are not, but *anyone* can learn to speak in public.

People often ask me how I get over my nerves prior to speaking in public. I always have a bit of a laugh because really, I never do. As Dale Carnegie said, *'There are always three speeches for every one that you actually gave. The one you practiced, the one you gave, and the one you wish you gave.'* This is very true for me and for every speaker that I know.

So, while most of us will never be able to fully and completely let go of our nerves, we can learn to speak with confidence and clarity. And that means that we can all, ultimately, learn how to present with impact.

Why does presenting matter?

The world is noisy. Today we're extremely interconnected, which means we receive data from across the world easily and all the time. In fact, the number of emails sent and received globally *per day* in 2021 was 319.6 billion.[1] All this noise means that we're trying to do more with less. This is particularly true for consultants and thought leaders.

But this interconnected world also has some strong benefits. In 2022, 200 million people joined the internet giving it a global usage of five billion people in total.[2] Other statistics show that this new digital world means that by 2025 nearly half the world's population will be self-employed.[3]

As consultants, thought leaders, coaches or people who are otherwise self-employed, this interconnected community is a huge benefit. It means that I don't need to be local for people to buy 'me'. I can be face-

---

1   Ceci, L. (22 August 2023). 'Number of sent and received e-mails per day worldwide from 2017 to 2025 (in billions).' Statista. Accessed at https://www.statista.com/statistics/456500/daily-number-of-e-mails-worldwide/.

2   (27 April 2022). 'More Than 5 Billion People Now Use the Internet.' We Are Social. Accessed at https://wearesocial.com/au/blog/2022/04/more-than-5-billion-people-now-use-the-internet/.

3   Thingbø, G. (23 July 2022). 'The workplace of 2025: a reflection on IDC's predictions.' Kinly. Accessed at https://blog.kinly.com/the-workplace-of-2025-a-reflection-on-idc-predictions.

to-face and 'virtually' local to people across the globe. And it's my ability to communicate and present well that allows me to access and engage with that online community for the best results.

Presenting well means that I can show up in Facebook Live videos and video blogs. I can communicate through reels and podcasts. And I can, of course, continue to undertake traditional presenting in keynotes and through other speaking events. These online and in-person ways of connecting provide more and varied opportunities to reach your target audience which ultimately enables you to stand out from the crowd.

Skills for the future include communication

The Future Work Skills 2020 Report from the Institute For The Future tells us that there are 10 key skills and six drivers for the future of work.[4] Three of the key skills identified in the report are:

1. Sense-making, which is the ability to understand and explain experiences;

2. Social intelligence, which is understanding how social interaction works (like emotional intelligence on steroids); and

3. New-media literacy (fluency in all forms of communication), which helps people learn quickly. We will see a break away from information being statically presented (such as through PowerPoint slides) and a move towards more immersive and visually stimulating content (such as video).

---

4   Davies, A, Fiddler, D & Gorbis, M. (2011). 'Future Work Skills 2020.' Institute for the Future for the University of Phoenix Research Institute. Accessed at https://legacy.iftf.org/futureworkskills/.

Boris Groysberg, professor of business administration at Harvard Business School and author of *Talk, Inc.*, spent time helping top-tier senior search consultants place executives in global roles in 2010. He was able to identify new skills for today's modern business leaders – and one of the most important he discovered was a person's ability to present.

In fact, Groysberg determined that being able to speak at conferences and events would be one of the key proficiencies for senior executives. It's interesting to note that these consultants represented a wide range of industries, across 19 countries.

So – as the research is demonstrating – the ability to communicate, sell and market yourself is a vital part of having a successful practice in the future. We also know that clients consume a lot of information and make many decisions prior to contacting us. Data from Forrester Research tells us that up to 90% of a buying decision is complete before a customer even calls a supplier – and the internet is a huge part of that.[5]

The more information we can share with our audience and the more trust we can build, the more likely we're going to be able to build our practice. If we don't, we aren't able to differentiate ourselves from the competition. Instead, we become commoditised and people will decide to work with us based only on price because that's the only identifiable differentiator. But if we can show them our unique points of difference by sharing with our audience, they can choose to work with us because we better align with their values, we offer a better service, our customers are happier or something else altogether.

---

5   Lecinski, J. (August 2014). 'ZMOT: Why It Matters Now More Than Ever.' Think with Google. Accessed at https://www.thinkwithgoogle.com/marketing-strategies/search/zmot-why-it-matters-now-more-than-ever/.

Our customers are going to pigeonhole us, however, for one aspect or another. So, if they're going to pigeonhole us, we have to ensure that we are being correctly identified. If we're pigeonholed in the wrong category, as the wrong speaker, or in the wrong market, then a customer cannot find us to buy us.

We need to ensure this doesn't happen. And our marketing communications – including our presenting – helps us to differentiate ourselves. We can become known as an expert in a certain niche or as a particular style of speaker in a specific category. In this way can we amplify the value that we bring.

Mastering exceptional speaking

Being able to stand confidently in front of your audience and speak or present well is a cornerstone of your practice's success. However, it's not enough to just *be* a speaker. The true differentiator lies in elevating your presentation skills from merely good to exceptional.

Exceptional speaking transcends the basics of clear communication and engaging delivery. It goes further, creating a deep connection with your audience. It involves having a profound understanding of their needs and expectations. And the ability to convey your message in a way that resonates on a personal and impactful level.

Exceptional speakers are those who not only inform but inspire. This level of speaking requires a blend of skills – a mastery of the subject, an empathetic engagement with the audience and a dynamic presentation style that adapts to the people in the room. Exceptional speakers don't just speak. They create experiences that linger in the minds of their listeners long after the speech has concluded.

> Exceptional speaking transcends the basics of clear communication and engaging delivery. It goes further, creating a deep connection with your audience.

When you become an exceptional speaker it, in turn, ignites interest and enthusiasm in your listeners. It transforms a standard presentation into a memorable and influential experience that can cause your listeners to take the action that you want them to take, whether that's to work with you, make a change in their own method of working or something else entirely.

But becoming an exceptional speaker requires you to become a proficient speaker, and then to take that to the next level. It requires continuous learning, practicing and refining of your skills. And it also requires you to be vulnerable enough to be open to feedback so that you can continue to grow and develop and better connect with your audiences.

Ultimately, exceptional speaking is a powerful tool. In fact, it's one of the most powerful tools that you have to enhance your professional practice. That's because it's not just about conveying information. It's about influencing perspectives, changing minds and inspiring action. And it's these skills that will allow you to position yourself not just as a speaker, but as an impactful leader in your field.

Our Australian challenges to speaking

We do have a couple of particularly Australian challenges to becoming speakers (and, by extension, exceptional speakers) – 'the tall poppy' syndrome and natural Australian scepticism.

The 'tall poppy' syndrome

In Australia, we have what is known as the 'tall poppy' syndrome, which gives us a subconscious belief that it's not cool to stand out. It's not cool to say, 'Look at me. I'm great at what I do.'

This impacts many people even in business. In fact, I find a lot of people see marketing and personal branding as a narcissistic, look-at-me approach to building their business, which puts them off from really investing the time and energy into it. But I don't think it's about that at all. It's not about being a tall poppy or showing off. It's about being able to connect, inspire and engage your audience.

Marketing yourself is not self-serving. You aren't looking to put the attention on yourself. Instead, it's about your client. It's about helping your audience. You need to be really clear about who you are so that they can connect with that. Our ability to communicate and present well helps us to stand out and sell ourselves without attention seeking or chest beating. Our audience sees that we are sharing valuable information and insights that can help them. We aren't standing out to show off. We're standing out to demonstrate how we can help.

Australian scepticism

The second challenge that we face as presenters in Australia is our natural Australian scepticism. As a speaker I've often found that Australian audiences don't necessarily appear captivated or watch us like they're excited. This means that as speakers, we have to work hard to cut through that and to get them onside. Overseas conference audiences, in particular the US market, are far more enthusiastic about what we have to say. In fact, you will be likely to get a standing ovation there! When we present to any audience we need to match the energy the audience has and take the energy to where we need it to go. You need to be both informative and entertaining!

But just because the energy is different doesn't mean that we aren't getting through. Really connecting with the unique needs of our audience can help us get there.

Making exceptional speaking part of your business growth strategy

As an expert or consultant, it's important to understand where exceptional speaking sits in the context of business growth. From my experience, most experts find it hard to incorporate speaking as part of their business in general, and exceptional speaking often seems totally out of reach.

However, speaking, whether through conversation or presentation, is one of the best ways that trusted leaders can power their business growth. Clients want to hear from you. Your communication creates trust and accountability. It helps them to learn about the essence of you. And it helps them to intuit whether they want to work with you.

When you speak, you're breathing life into your written words and inviting your clients to live the experience with you. If you can do that, then it's going to create a really high impact. And your business and practice are going to stand out far more.

Exceptional speaking is a powerful growth tool, but it's equally important to manage the business side of your speaking practice so that you commercialise your work. Mastering the business of speaking is what

"

Exceptional
speaking is a
powerful growth tool,
but it's equally important to
manage the business side of
your speaking practice so
that you commercialise
your work.

"

transforms you from a good speaker to a sought-after professional, and until you do this, you won't be able to make speaking part of your business growth strategy. Not to worry – we'll cover the business of speaking in Exceptional Commerciality, Chapter 6.

What I love about speaking as part of a business growth strategy is that you get to reach and connect with a lot of people reasonably quickly (Matt Church describes this as 'paid distribution'). You might be asking, 'How do I get more clients? How do I get in front of more people? How do I build databases?' Well, speaking is one of the most efficient ways for you to do all of those things. If you're speaking on a topic, your audience inherently understands that you must know something about the subject, so it positions you as an expert.

Sometimes people who have personally branded businesses hope that they'll be discovered as a result of a Google search. However, Google searches are really tailored to answer a specific question (and without any further input from you). On the other hand, speaking allows you to meet an audience wherever they are and whatever their questions are in a truly tailored way. In this way speaking is one of the most powerful things that you can do to build your personally branded business.

So how do you incorporate 'exceptional speaking' into your business, in a practical way? This means talking to people so they understand you are the person their business needs. When you present and speak, you will articulate what that challenge is for them, and that can often compel them to get in touch with you.

I often talk about using speaking as a tool for awareness and education. You can think of your speaking reach in terms of four quadrants of audience awareness.

From expert to influencer – marketing for growth

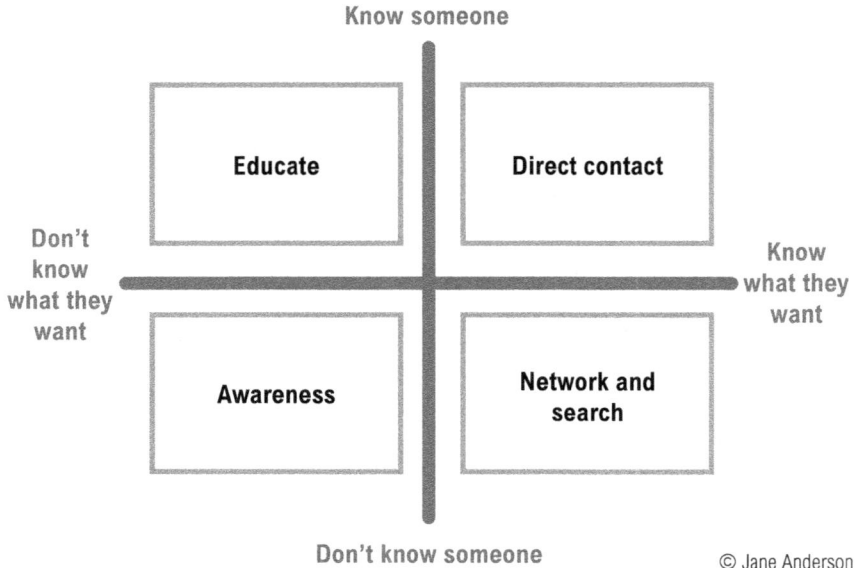

Know someone

Don't know what they want | Know what they want

Educate

Direct contact

Awareness

Network and search

Don't know someone

© Jane Anderson

1. **Direct contact.** The first quadrant is about direct contact. This is where people know you and know what they want. These are people who are going to remember your name, understand the work you do and the value you provide, and will consider working with you when they are looking for someone who offers the services you do.

   In this quadrant, your presentation is designed to influence and persuade your audience to take the next step. You may do this via your database – for example, by creating video blogs that go out via your newsletters. You may also do this when you are presenting to a group as part of your sales funnel. Perhaps you are hosting a breakfast or other event that feeds into the programs that you're delivering. Whatever the approach, you're taking the audience from knowing you to buying you.

2. **Network reach.** The second quadrant is about network reach. This network or 'fetch' quadrant is where the audience has never heard of you before. They don't know who you are, but they need someone who offers the services that you do.

    In this quadrant, you've likely had this person referred to you. For example, you might have spoken at an event where somebody heard you and then referred you to someone else. Or you might have posted a video of your presentation or speech online. In that case, someone may have found you via an online search on Google or YouTube.

    Here you might also want to think about your search engine optimisation (SEO) work because it's important that you are easily found. You want to be found from keywords such as 'best speaker on X topic', for example.

3. **Awareness.** The third quadrant is about awareness. This quadrant is where keynote speaking finds its place, and where it becomes a big driver for your practice. It will put you in an excellent position to tailor your speaking to either sell or build your database because through keynote speaking you may be getting in front of new audiences who you have never met before. This is also where understanding your business strategy as a speaker becomes critical. Whether it's designing your collateral, refining your message or building client relationships, the business of speaking keeps your name in front of the people who matter.

In this quadrant, you may be asked to speak at a conference with an audience full of your ideal clients. Or you may be presenting as part of a webcast. Here you are casting a wide net, but the readiness of this market is generally reasonably low. So more often than not they won't buy straight away, unless they're in a highly-targeted market, you deliver a spot-on message or you offer a lower price point.

4. **Push.** The fourth and final quadrant is the push quadrant. This quadrant is about education, and this is where you are creating content such as video blogs, podcasts or presentations as part of your lead generation activity. Here you are generally speaking to people who follow you, but you are looking to educate them in order to build trust.

Speaking can also help your business by:

- Putting you in front of new audiences who you may not have previously considered as potential clients.

- Helping you to receive feedback and get a sense of the challenges faced by potential clients.

- Communicating any pivots or repositioning your business has done within the industry. (When I had positioned my business too hard into a particular market, one of my mentors, Matt Church, said, 'Right, you've repositioned and now what you need to do is go and speak somewhere every week.')

- Allowing you to leverage the presentation for a variety of other uses. For example, you could record it and use it for YouTube videos.

- Creating more commercial opportunities to leverage growth and revenue.

Do it to master it

Understanding why exceptional speaking matters is the first step. The next is to take some action. If you want to know how you can double your impact, engagement and influence, and take your presentations from boring to brilliant, I have just one answer – hone your craft.

As experts, we really should be speaking somewhere most weeks. When I first started, I found it hard to get in front of people and still have the 40 sales meetings I needed each week. However I realised that if I could have only one keynote and speak for just an hour a week, then I would be reaching and engaging with these same people in a more effective and efficient way. And that was certainly what happened!

One of my coaches, Neil McCallum, of the Million Dollar Salon, once said to me, 'OK, go away now and do 200 keynotes and then come back and talk to me.' He knew that this practice would help me to learn and hone the basic speaking skills that I needed. And practise will certainly do the same for you.

Now if you don't have a personally branded business yet, but are thinking about becoming a consultant, a thought leader or an expert in your field, you can start speaking at any time. One of the best things about speaking is that you can do it even before you leave your day job or corporate career. It allows you to jump-start your practice while still being able to keep your steady income.

> One of the best things about speaking is that you can do it even before you leave your day job or corporate career. It allows you to jump-start your practice while still being able to keep your steady income.

Seek advice from mentors

I used to go out and watch speakers in person or on YouTube and think, 'Wow, they're just so inspiring. How is it that they do that? I don't think I'm very inspiring. I'm just really practical. I just focus on what will get the results and what will work. How boring!'

And so, I struggled with trying to work out how I was going to be able to do this well. How was I going to be a world-class speaker? I didn't feel that I had anything truly interesting or unique to set me apart. I haven't climbed Mount Everest. I haven't recovered from cancer. I've got all my limbs. I worried that perhaps I didn't have anything that was good enough. I just didn't know how to take my speaking to the next level.

I decided to do something about it. I decided to go and find five people who I thought were good speakers. The benchmark that I set for each speaker was that they were generating more than a million dollars a year from their speaking. I wanted to learn from these people because I thought that if they were generating that kind of money, they must be doing it right.

After finding these five speakers, I got them to mentor, train and teach me. I spent a fortune on learning – around $40k trying to understand how speaking works and how the speaking industry works.

My first port of call was Neil McCallum, whose Million Dollar Salon program teaches hair salons how to grow their businesses. He taught me storytelling.

The second person I learned from was Catherine Palin-Brinkworth. She listened to me speak and gave me invaluable feedback. Catherine has been the president of the Global Speakers Federation and was kind enough to spend some time with me and help me improve. I'm always indebted to her for her feedback, particularly being female.

Keith Abraham is another person who has been valuable to me (we'll hear more from him in Chapter 7). He's a certified speaking professional and has been in the business for more than 30 years. Keith is a mentor to a large number of speakers globally. He's also an expert on achievement and speaks on productivity, passion, goal setting and business growth.

Keith really is extraordinary and known as the true gentleman of speakers. When I went to see him, I didn't have any money to pay for any guidance, so I offered to do anything I could to help him. And what I did was help him with his marketing strategy on LinkedIn. I was fortunate enough to be able to help him grow his practice, and lucky enough to have him help me elevate my speaking and presenting. And we've been wonderful friends ever since.

My next amazing mentor is Rowdy McLean, another well-regarded global speaker. Rowdy has been speaking for 25 years and is a certified speaking professional. He is an expert in playing a bigger game and helping people to expand their thinking. Rowdy has been a real sounding board in helping me to grow my practice.

In recent years, I've had the immense pleasure of working with Dr Louise Mahler (who we also hear from in Chapter 7). Louise is a master speaker, with a background as an operatic performer gracing the stages all over Europe. With that experience and such obvious skillful performances on stage, it's easy to think that Louise has it all figured out. But she too suffers from performance anxiety. And it was learning from her that helped me to push past many aspects of my own anxiety. More importantly, it was such a relief to see that even incredible presenters can struggle with such problems. I was certainly not alone!

Last, but certainly not least, is Matt Church, one of the top 10 global speakers booked internationally. Matt's also been ranked in the top 10 motivational speakers and named Australian Speaker of the Year. Renowned for his expertise in thought leadership and motivational leadership, Matt has a wonderful program called Speakership, where he works with some of the best speakers in the country. It's been incredible to learn from him.

One of the biggest lessons I learned from my mentors was that speaking isn't just about being great on stage – it's about mastering the business side of speaking as well. This was a big learning curve, but one that made the difference between getting occasional gigs and having a strong speaking career.

I am grateful for all of my mentors' support, guidance and help and for pushing me to become a better speaker. I've gone on to coach, mentor and train a number of professional speakers since. My expertise has helped them to better market and position themselves so they can grow their practices from the stage.

In my practice, I don't just focus on my speaking. I'm also obsessed with helping people connect so that they have enough impact in their communications to help the people they want to help.

Six types of speakers

To become an exceptional speaker you must first understand the kind of speaker you are now. To do that I use my Exceptional Speaker Model. And when I'm working with people, I'm looking for where they are on this scale.

Exceptional Speaker Model

	Type	Focus	0% IMPACT
You	Rockstar	Fun	100
	Engager	Conviction	75
	Practicer	Presence	50
Them	Regurgitator	Insights	25
	Reader	Preparation	0
	Refuser	Purpose	-5

© Jane Anderson

As you can see, there are six rungs. The three lower rungs tend to be speakers who are focusing on themselves. To advance to the three higher rungs, you need to be thinking about your audience and the experience for them.

To climb up the ladder you need to understand where you currently sit on the scale. Are you a Refuser, a Reader, a Regurgitator, a Practiser, an Engager or a Rockstar?

The Refuser

The speaker at the very bottom of the ladder is a 'Refuser'. A 'Refuser' does not understand the reason for speaking. They don't see what the benefit would be. They need a reason for why speaking would be valuable to them – beyond just gaining confidence in front of a group.

The focus at this level is a sense of purpose. The Refuser has to have some kind of purpose, a reason why. How is speaking going to help them contribute to their vision and their goals and what they're trying to achieve? At this level, the amount of impact that they're having is generally very low (even negative). There are opportunities out there but they're not coming to them because they're not putting themselves out there or making themselves sufficiently visible.

To be able to move in the right direction as a speaker you need to link your speaking to your purpose. What's the point? Is it going to help you to get more clients? Is it about getting promotions? Or is it about actually becoming a speaker? Even if you're an intern, it might be about adding speaking to your resume.

The Reader

The second level is the 'Reader'. This is somebody for whom speaking is just reading content from a slide. More often than not, a 'Reader' has not adequately prepared. So they've just put all the information onto a presentation in front of them. In fact, often they've just copied and pasted everything out of reports. And even though the content is likely accurate, the delivery is certainly uninteresting and unengaging.

If you're a 'Reader', at this point you need to focus on preparing to speak. The amount of impact that you're having at this level is generally zero. Rather than standing out you're blending in because presenting in this way has become the norm in corporate and business settings. People who are 'Readers' sometimes have a fear of making something interesting or engaging because nobody else does it that way. They don't want to feel like they're putting their neck out for other people to criticise them.

I do get a lot of people who say to me, 'Oh I can speak off the cuff. You know? I don't need to prepare.' Michael Port, author of *Book Yourself Solid*,[6] said, 'Show me somebody who puts together a presentation at the last minute, or speaks off the cuff, and I'll show you someone who's procrastinated till the last minute.'

So for 'Readers' preparation is key. You really need to invest the time in preparing and rehearsing. The amount of impact that you're having as a speaker when just reading slides is really not a lot. The audience can do that by themselves. You might as well send the presentation out and not speak at all.

The Regurgitator

Level three is the 'Regurgitator'. This person is just repeating content that they've been given. If you're a 'Regurgitator' you're generally being asked to, or choosing to, deliver something that you haven't created. This might be content that you found elsewhere or even developed using AI. Whatever the case, this is not your own thought leadership.

---

6   Port, M. (2017). *Book Yourself Solid: The Fastest, Easiest, and Most Reliable System for Getting More Clients Than You Can Handle Even if You Hate Marketing*. Wiley.

Someone who's a 'Regurgitator' hasn't provided any new insights. They're not offering a new lens of interpretation or original thought. They're simply feeding back content that's already out there.

If you're currently a 'Regurgitator', in order to move forward in your speaking (and your impact) you need to really focus on giving your content some insights. It's not just about providing the research and evidence and data. It's about proving a new way of thinking about that research, evidence and data.

Ask yourself – what does this mean? Why is that? How does this impact your audience or connect to their world? When you're actively giving insight into your content, you're probably about a quarter of the way into having some impact with your presentations.

The Practiser

Level four is the 'Practiser'. This is somebody who has rehearsed their speaking to perfection. The problem? While their presentation might be flawless, they're not actually engaging people. It's obvious that they have practised endlessly, but there's no connection with the audience, no pauses, no intonation. They're not mindful of the audience, or even paying attention to their reactions. I'm big on practising, but over-practising can result in a speaker being stuck in their own world. Their attention will be on themselves and they will lose their connection with the audience.

If you're a 'Practiser' you're trying so hard to be so perfect that it actually looks fake. You become so fixated on a perfect delivery for the audience that you fail to give them an experience. The way to create an experience is to create presence. So to have real presence is to be present with the audience and attuned to what's going on for them.

If you want to move on from being a 'Practiser', your real focus should be around presence. Instead of focusing inward, look outward. Consider what's going on in the room. Who's in the room? What's their experience like? What type of mood is in the room? If you stay at the 'Practiser' level your impact is probably only 50% of what's possible.

The Engager

Level five is somebody who is an 'Engager'. I generally say this is somebody good at connecting with the audience. When they're speaking, they're thinking about their audience, and they're mindful of the experience for them. They may be trying to connect with them a little bit too much and may be feeling a little bit insecure, but they're reaching out and engaging.

If you're an 'Engager' you're already good at asking questions. So, if you're at this point, what you need to be mindful of is understanding what you are doing with your engaged audience. What is the actual intent of the presentation? What is the purpose behind it? What are you trying to get people to do as the next step?

To move on from this level, you've got to have a lot of conviction. You need to know who it is that you're trying to influence and what message you're trying to persuade them to accept. As an 'Engager' the amount of impact you have is at about 75% of what's possible. But getting to the next level is the goal.

The Rockstar

And now we arrive at the very top of the ladder – level six. This is somebody I like to call a 'Rockstar' because they make presenting *with impact* look really easy. They engage, they entertain, they inform and they persuade.

From the audience's perspective, the time goes fast when they're with a 'Rockstar'. They may be having fun or be totally captivated – so much so that they don't even notice the time. They actually don't want it to be over. They want more.

The 'Rockstar' makes this engagement look easy because they've done all the work before ever setting foot on the stage. They're like an iceberg – from the surface it looks like it's come together easily, but there's so much work lying underneath. But all the work a 'Rockstar' has done to prepare, practise and hone their craft means that now it's about having a great time. And while they're presenting they're really just enjoying it.

I remember being at a P!nk concert many years ago (she truly is a Rockstar!). She was singing while performing flawless aerial theatrics, suspended from the ceiling using a harness, bands and wires. She made the moves look easy – but behind the scenes there were hours and hours of rehearsal that would have gone into it.

Just like P!nk, at this level you have everything going on, but you make it look so easy. And you're able to engage *and* persuade, and get people to do what you want them to do. You're at 100% impact. And you truly are a 'Rockstar'.

"

Connection
is simply about making
the experience in the
room about the audience
– as opposed to being
all about you.

"

Content, connection, collateral, commerciality

To move up the Exceptional Speaker Scale you need to refocus your energies. I want to share four elements that you need to consider to be able to move to that 'Rockstar' status:

1. Exceptional content

The first one is your content. That probably sounds obvious, but you've got to know what you're talking about and have conviction around it.

You also want to make sure that your content is about 'brand you'. In other words, it's about where you want to go in your practice, and what you want to be known for. If you're speaking on content that you don't want to be known for, then that's not good positioning and you'll just be wasting your time.

You need to really consider your content, and understand what your message is. Whittle it down to the main elements. Consider the three key points that you want your audience to take away, but never forget the overall message that you're trying to get across.

2. Exceptional connection

The second element to consider is around connection. When it comes to speaking and presenting, there's often a real barrier between you and your audience. Your job is to try to break that barrier so that you feel connected to them, and, most importantly, that they feel connected to you. Whatever the energy is in the room, you need to recognise that, and manage it.

The elements that will help you to connect are things like humour and storytelling. It could be research or case studies. It could even be how you use your body, your gestures or how you dress. It can be all sorts of things.

Connection is simply about making the experience in the room about the audience – as opposed to being all about you. And rather than dictating content to them, it should feel like you're working together towards a common goal.

3. Exceptional collateral

The third element is your collateral. These are all the things that support you to be able to get your message across. They are often your words – brochures, whitepapers, books and other handouts, for example. But they can also be how you dress or how you look, how you speak or what you say.

One of the things I often find when I'm reviewing someone's collaterals – particularly slides – is that they've got way too much content on there. They will often have three different graphs or multiple models all describing the same thing.

When it comes to your collateral – particularly your visual collateral – you need to really simplify what's on your screen. And it's vital that you make sure that your collateral matches your message. This is so your verbal message matches the message on your screen and people can easily understand what you're talking about and why it matters to them.

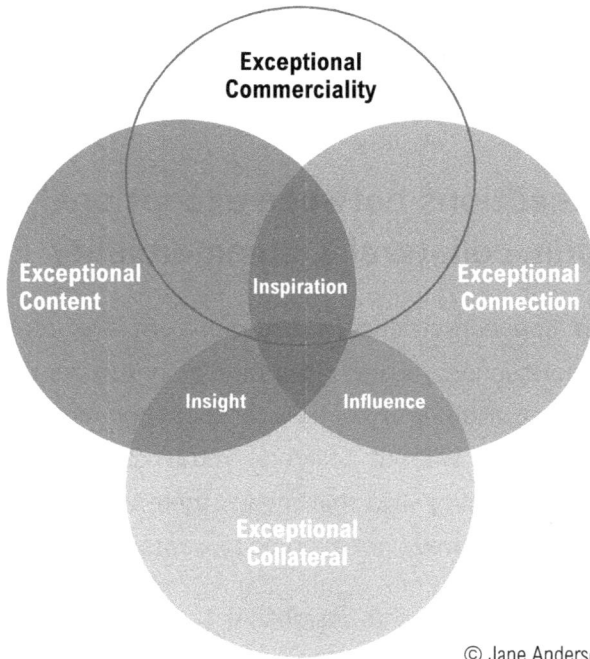

© Jane Anderson

4. Exceptional commerciality

The fourth and final element is your commerciality. This is essentially the business of speaking or understanding how to turn your speaking into a sustainable business. Of course, delivering a compelling and impactful presentation is important, but it's meaningless if you can't turn it into a commercial win. Many talented speakers fall into the trap of focusing solely on the craft of speaking while neglecting the business side of the equation. Without a commercial mindset, your work (and you as well!) might risk being a well-spoken secret rather than a sought-after expert.

To grow your practice and revenue with speaking you need to price and position yourself strategically, market your brand, leverage your speaking engagements, generate leads and focus on building your list and your relationships. This will allow you to create business opportunities beyond the stage.

The intersections between exceptional content, connection, collateral & commerciality

Content and connection lead to inspiration. At the intersection of content and connection, you get inspiration. Here you get the moments of brilliance that allow you to truly build a connection with your messaging. However, without collateral you'll have nothing visual to back up your messaging. And that means there's a lot of pressure on you to perform. And frankly, not everybody wants to – or can – do that.

Content and collateral lead to insight. At the intersection of content and collateral, you get insight. It's here that you get an accurate and deep understanding of your audience, which allows you to create more aligned messaging and deliver it with greater impact. On the other hand, if you are missing connection, people will just find you boring. They won't feel inspired or engaged.

Connection and collateral lead to influence. At the intersection of connection and collateral, you get influence. This is hugely important when you are looking to create impact with your speaking and presentations. But, if you're focusing on connection, trying to make the whole experience fun, and you've got some cool collateral, but you haven't really thought about your key message in your content, it all just feels fragmented. In this situation people aren't going to remember what you said.

Commerciality overarches all other connections & leads to increase

We can think of commerciality as the thread that ties the other elements together and gives you exceptional speaking purpose. You can have exceptional content, connection and collateral, but if none of it leads to opportunities and growth, or more revenue and leads, then you're not building a sustainable speaking practice.

Commerciality is what ensures all your efforts and work on the stage converts to fantastic business outcomes off the stage. It's the strategy that turns inspiration into insight, insight into influence and influence into growth in terms of your reach and your revenue so that your presentations truly become part of your pipeline.

To be impactful, you need content, connection, collateral & commerciality

To be a truly impactful presenter, you must have all four elements – content, connection, collateral *and* commerciality, which will give you inspiration, insight, influence *and* increase. Your audience will know that you understand them, that you're the right person to help them and they'll remember you. They'll be able to see themselves in the world that you're offering.

In my practice and in my speaking I very much come from a place of help rather than hustle. Speaking is a selling technique, but if it's done right, it doesn't feel salesy. It shows that you are there to help, that you're there to make change and that you're ready to act in the listeners' interests. Most importantly it shows your audience that you are the right person to do all those things.

The war on boring

I've got a bit of a war on boring. We don't want boring keynotes. We don't want boring speeches. We don't want boring presentations. We've got to make them fun, interesting and engaging. Even more than engaging, we've got to make them captivating.

Of course that's hard when you are under pressure, but you can do it by managing your time. When I've got a keynote coming up, I block out time in my calendar not only for my preparation, but also for my rehearsal. And if I haven't delivered a particular presentation before, I block out more time.

When I'm preparing and rehearsing, I also make sure that I'm using some engaging techniques, to keep it interesting and focused on connection. And in order to ensure that it's all in there, I need the time set aside. Otherwise it would just be slapped together at the last minute.

Before any presentation, think about your content, your collateral and how you are going to connect with people. Arm yourself with information. If you work with local business owners, see if you can have a chat with your local chamber of commerce. Or survey your community. Find out how you can add value to their businesses and lives.

Then look for ways that you can start practicing it. Practise on friends, practise on family. If you've got a dog, practise on the dog. Anything that will help you get your confidence up is worth it. But the most important thing is just to start somewhere.

Conclusion

In this book I've brought together all the things you need to focus on to give you the outcomes you're looking for – that is, to become an exceptional speaker who delivers truly impactful presentations.

But the main goal is to learn the best way to plan and design a structured and professional presentation in a way that will best grab the attention of your audience and influence them to take action. These high-impact presentations help your audience remember your key message. And they give you the ability to conquer your own inhibitions and the influence to be able to sell from the stage.

CHAPTER 2

WHAT ARE EXCEPTIONAL SPEAKERS & IMPACTFUL PRESENTATIONS

'The goal of effective communication should be for listeners to say "Me too!" versus "So what?"'

— Jim Rohn

Now that we've discussed why exceptional speaking that leads to real impact is important, we need to learn what makes someone an exceptional speaker and what leads to an impactful presentation.

We've established that 'Rockstar' status is our aim. And to be a 'Rockstar' you have to make three elements work for you – knowing your content, connecting with your audience and creating strong collateral.

When you have these three elements you know what you're talking about, you're able to find ways to engage the hearts and minds of your audience and you're able to support and enhance your message.

You're then in a good place to make real impact and see real change. Your audience isn't just going to listen to you. They're going to be captivated by you. They're going to be inspired by you. They're going to be learning from you. And, most importantly, they're going to want to know more from you. This gives you influence, and people will be willing to buy from you.

Once people want to know more from you, you're then in an excellent position to encourage them to take the next steps with you (which is all part of the business of speaking!). Maybe you want their contact information for your list. Maybe you want them to buy your product or attend your workshop. Maybe you have a course that could help change their business or their life. Whatever outcome you're looking for, you want to encourage your audience to follow your lead, and take that next step with you. This is high impact speaking.

But before we can dig into the details of content, connection and collateral, we need to determine what actually makes an exceptional speaker and an impactful presentation.

What makes an exceptional speaker?

To begin to develop our own exceptional speaking abilities we first have to understand the difference between a speaker and an *exceptional* speaker.

SPEAKER	EXCEPTIONAL SPEAKER
Content-focused	Connection-focused
Delivering information	Building emotion
Focused on themselves	Focused on audience
Practises	Rehearses

1. A speaker is focused on content; an *exceptional* speaker is focused on connection.

A speaker prioritises the content that they'll be delivering. They spend time ensuring that they're delivering all the relevant information, data and facts. They concentrate on their material with the idea that the main value of their presentation is in giving the information.

On the other hand, an exceptional speaker understands that their true power when presenting lies in making a connection with their audience. While they also craft content, they do it with the mindset that it needs to resonate on a personal level with the audience. They do this by weaving in stories, anecdotes and real-world examples. By doing this a speaker becomes an exceptional speaker because they transform a one-way information dump into an interactive experience that fosters a meaningful connection with their audience.

> For the exceptional speaker, the presentation is a dynamic experience – a dialogue rather than a monologue.

2. A speaker is focused on delivering information; an *exceptional* speaker is focused on building emotion.

A speaker understands the need to deliver information and is focused on creating a straightforward transmission of knowledge from themselves to their audience. In other words, their goal is to inform. And, most importantly, to accurately inform. They have set their content, and now the goal is simply to get that content to the audience.

An exceptional speaker, however, understands that just giving the information is not enough. They realise that evoking emotions is the key to making their message memorable. Because of that they learn to use their words, tone, body language and gestures to build inspiration, empathy, excitement or urgency. And then by tapping emotions they create lasting impact that touches both the minds *and* hearts of the audience.

3. A speaker is focused on themselves; an *exceptional* speaker is focused on the audience.

A speaker concentrates on their own performance. They focus on polishing how they sound, look and move and are preoccupied with perfecting their delivery technique. Because of that they tend to stick rigidly to their script, and sometimes that means they fail to take into account what's going on in the room.

Exceptional speakers shift the focus from themselves to their audience. They pay close attention to their delivery to the audience so they can adjust their structure, tone, pace and content to maintain real-time engagement and interest. This also means paying attention to what's going on around their audience and to their audience.

For the exceptional speaker, the presentation is a dynamic experience – a dialogue rather than a monologue. Cicero, the great ancient Roman orator, developed what is known today as the five canons of rhetoric. His final canon is 'delivery' which is the actual performance and use of gestures, projection, articulation and eye contact. Cicero understood that the experience must be dynamic to be impactful.

4. A speaker is focused on practising; an *exceptional* speaker is focused on rehearsing.

Most speakers will take the time to practise their presentations and speeches. In fact, almost all will practise multiple times and some will even prepare until they know the material by heart. This type of preparation is necessary, of course. But its focus tends to be about getting comfortable with the material itself.

An exceptional speaker doesn't just practise – they rehearse. They get up off their chair and create a space that will simulate the actual speaking environment. They consider various audience reactions and refine the information and the delivery. They rehearse with purpose, focused on the flow of speech, pauses, emphasis, how to use the stage and how to prepare for different audience dynamics. It was the incredible actress Julie Andrews who said, *'The amateur works until he can get it right. The professional works til he can't get it wrong.'*

This approach means that when the exceptional speaker steps on stage they're not just reciting information – they're delivering an experience.

What makes an impactful presentation?

One of the most highly impactful presentations I've ever seen was Mhairi Black's maiden speech to the Scottish Parliament. In this speech she discussed the government's approach to unemployment and the growing need for food banks. Mhairi's speech was widely praised, and viewed on various media over 10 million times.[7] It's also been described as 'outstanding', 'principled' and 'passionate' by SNP Parliamentary Group Leader, Angus Robertson.[8] So what made her presentation so impactful?

Part of what made Mhairi Black's speech so incredible was her age. At only 20 years old she was the youngest member of parliament when she made her maiden speech. She began by using humour to break the ice around the elephant in the room (her young age). This early acknowledgement allowed her to effectively remove the barrier between herself and the audience. And that cleared a pathway so her message could get through.

Once Mhairi had broken the ice, she acknowledged her opponent, the people in the room and their history. This set the scene and demonstrated to the audience that she understood the importance of their shared past. Then she used storytelling, to share about a gentleman she had gotten to know while working at a charitable organisation.

---

7   (19 July 2015). 'Mhairi Black's maiden speech tops 10m online views.' *BBC News*. Accessed at https://www.bbc.com/news/uk-scotland-scotland-politics-33585087.
8   Mhairi Black's maiden speech. BBC News.

About him, Mhairi said:

> *Before I was elected, I volunteered for a charitable organisation. There was a gentleman who I grew very fond of. He was one of these guys who has been battered by life in every way imaginable. You name it, he's been through it. And he used to come in to get food from this charity, and it was the only food that he had access to and it was the only meal he would get. And I sat with him and he told me about his fear of going to the Job Centre. He said, 'I've heard the stories Mhairi, they try and trick you out, they'll tell you you're a liar. I'm not a liar Mhairi, I'm not.' And I told him, 'It's OK, calm down. Go, be honest, it'll be fine.'*
>
> *I then didn't see him for about two or three weeks. I did get very worried, and when he finally did come back in I said to him, 'How did you get on?'*
>
> *And without saying a word he burst into tears. That grown man standing in front of a 20-year-old crying his eyes out, because what had happened to him was the money that he would normally use to pay for his travel to come to the charity to get his food he decided that in order to afford to get to the Job Centre he would save that money. Because of this, he didn't eat for five days, he didn't drink. When he was on the bus on the way to the Job Centre he fainted due to exhaustion and dehydration. He was 15 minutes late for the Job Centre and he was sanctioned for 13 weeks.*

This story paved the way for Mhairi's message. She'd gotten their attention and made a connection, so could hit them between the eyes with her message, and that was that her constituency was struggling.

She used data and statistics to back up her points, and to illustrate the reality of life for her constituents, which included food insecurity and poverty.

The combination of elements made an incredible impact on those in the audience, and even those who have seen or read her speech in the years since. Mhairi's messaging had influence, so she could ultimately move the needle for her constituents.

Learnings from Mharie

So what do we learn from Mhairi's speech about what makes an impactful presentation?

1. Acknowledge the elephant in the room
2. Use humour (though this could be another unique trait)
3. Use storytelling
4. Engage your audience
5. Leverage other experts

Acknowledge the elephant in the room

Impactful speakers don't shy away from difficult conversations or confronting input. Take, for example, the situation where a team leader is giving a presentation about a new project that's about to start that will involve the entire team. Imagine she says that it will mean a few long days but that they'll have the support of the entire executive team. One of their team pipes up with a sarcastic comment like, 'Sure, just like always.'

Instead of addressing the (unspoken) concern that's being displayed here, the team leader just says, 'Yes, like always' and moves on because she doesn't want to deal with the underlying emotion behind the real words.

But her avoidance doesn't do her any favours. While having the conversation is hard, by avoiding it she loses credibility and trust with her team. Instead, she needs to point out the elephant in the room. She could say, 'I know that we've felt unsupported by the executives in the past. What do you think we could ask for this time that might help us get the support we need?'

This gives her credibility, builds her team's trust in her, and lets her address the real concerns that her team is facing.

When you're giving a presentation on stage you might not always get verbal feedback from the audience. But if you're aware that there is some particular worry, discontent or problem that is impacting the group, it almost always pays to address it.

Use humour

When it comes to getting your message across to an audience, humour has always been a fantastic tool. As French author Victor Hugo once said, 'Laughter is the sun that drives winter from the human face.' In other words, laughter makes people happy, engaged and light up from inside.

Importantly, when someone is humorous they come across as more likable. In fact, funny people are seen as more physically attractive and even as better potential mates.[9] But the end result is that when your audience likes you, they're going to be more open to your message.

A funny story is also just more interesting and engaging than a straight up recitation of information. It can provide emotional relief for the audience and help them to remember your points. Research shows that laughter can improve memory and cognitive function as well.[10]

Use storytelling

Storytelling is a vital part of your presentation skillset because, as humans, we naturally relate to them. Where people might drift off during a stream of facts or data, the structure of storytelling engages us (as it has for thousands of years). Stories evoke empathy and motivate the listener to take action.

And, because our brains seek and store information based on patterns, storytelling helps our audience to absorb and retain the information that we're presenting.[11]

Engage your audience

An audience that has to sit and listen for any length of time can get restless. When you're the speaker you'll know this is happening when

---

9   Tornquist, M & Chiappe, D. (12 October 2015). 'Effects of Humor Production, Humor Receptivity, and Physical Attractiveness on Partner Desirability.' *Evolutionary Psychology*. Accessed at https://journals.sagepub.com/doi/10.1177/1474704915608744.

10 Kennison, S. (2020). *The Cognitive Neuroscience of Humor*. American Psychological Association.

11 Willis, J. (12 September 2017). 'The Neuroscience of Narrative and Memory.' Edutopia. Accessed at https://www.edutopia.org/article/neuroscience-narrative-and-memory/.

you see people start to play with their phones, or whisper to colleagues. This is when you need to engage your audience.

When you're offering what seems to be a direct conversation between you and your audience, they feel engaged. Engaged audiences retain your ideas and insights. So how do you do this?

- *Focus your presentation on your audience* – Consider what they know about the topic, and what would be helpful for you to add to their knowledge. Then think about how you can best present the information to them to help them learn and understand.
- *Use an easy structure* – Too often speakers deliver information in too casual a way, almost like a brain dump or train of thought. But even though you want to be accessible in your delivery, you need to introduce it in a way that people can easily follow.
- *Get the audience involved* – From simple ice breakers to questions and answers, the more you can get your audience involved, the more energised and engaged they'll be with you.
- *Use innovative technology* – Think beyond the PowerPoint presentation which naturally lends itself to a static delivery of information. Instead, consider using tech to lay out all your main points, then get the audience to choose which topics they want to cover and in what order. You can also use video or music to increase interest and engagement.
- *Get participants on stage* – Whether other experts, or people from the audience, getting other people involved in your presentation will make it more interactive.

Leverage other experts

Just like Mhairi did in her speech, there is power in acknowledging and leveraging other experts. Whether you want to simply refer to the people that you admire and whose work has impacted your own, or bring other experts on stage to support your presentation, experts give you credibility and interest, and improve engagement.

What holds us back from becoming exceptional?

Feelings of inadequacy

Inadequacy is simply the feeling of not being good enough. You might feel that you don't have the experience, the following, the email list or something else entirely. But whatever it is, it stops you from believing that you have something important to add to the conversation, and that you can create impact.

I've written about this before – in my blogs, newsletters and books. But this is one of the most insidious things that holds us back from doing anything – including becoming an exceptional speaker.

Solutions for feelings of inadequacy

To get past feelings of inadequacy we need to build in feelings of self-worth and intrinsic value.[12] That is the way that we seek to feel adequate,

---

12   Neff, K. (January 2023). 'Self-Compassion: Theory, Method, Research, and Intervention.' *Annual Review of Psychology*. Accessed at https://www.annualreviews.org/doi/10.1146/annurev-psych-032420-031047.

to have positive views about ourselves and to feel good about who we are. When we have a positive self-view, we are also more likely to be happier, successful and even more popular.[13] And those feelings will allow us to expand our impact on the stage too.

Questions to ask yourself

If you're struggling with feelings of inadequacy, ask yourself:

1. Are these fears real – or are they ones I've created in my own mind?
2. Have I spoken to an expert, mentor or coach who has the experience to advise me?
3. Have I had a conversation with the decision-maker I'm hoping to influence, and shared what I'm trying to do and how I can help?

If you answered no to questions two and three, then you know what your next step should be!

Performance anxiety

Sometimes called 'stage fright', performance anxiety affects many people, including athletes, actors, musicians and public speakers. It's so common in fact that researchers suggest that 'most people would rather get the flu than perform' in front of others.[14]

---

13 Crocker, J & Knight, K. (August 2005). 'Contingencies of self-worth.' *Current directions in psychological science*. Accessed at https://journals.sagepub.com/doi/abs/10.1111/j.0963-7214.2005.00364.x.

14 Marks, H. (Rev'd by Bhandari, MD, S). Stage Fright (Performance Anxiety). (13 November 2021). WebMD. Accessed at https://www.webmd.com/anxiety-panic/guide/stage-fright-performance-anxiety.

Symptoms of performance anxiety are real and physical and can include:

- Rapid breathing
- Racing heart rate
- Dry mouth
- Tight throat
- Shaking or trembling
- Shaking or quaking voice and lips
- Sweating
- Cold hands
- Nausea
- Difficulty with vision (tunnel vision for example)[15]

The problem with performance anxiety is that it can prevent you from doing things that can substantially benefit your career (public speaking) and that you might in fact be very good at. It is also known to impact both your self-confidence and self-esteem[16] which can then leak into other aspects of your work, creating unnecessary stress and struggles.

---

15 Marks. Stage Fright.
16 Marks. Stage Fright.

Solutions for performance anxiety

1. **Rehearse.** The more prepared you are the better you'll feel.

2. **Eat well.** Limit caffeine and sugar on the day you're taking to the stage as this can give you a spike in energy that quickly drops. Eat a sensible meal a couple hours before you perform that includes complex carbohydrates and will keep you feeling satiated and energised.

3. **Get physical.** Burning off excess energy by taking a walk, doing some stretching or otherwise moving around can help ease anxious feelings before you take the stage. Stomping your feet to unjam your diaphragm can also really help.

4. **Focus on your audience.** Don't think about how you're feeling. Think about how your audience is feeling. Imagine them enjoying your speech and getting behind your message.

5. **Focus on the positive.** Don't dwell on negative thoughts and avoid thoughts that lead to self-doubt. Focus on the positive and visualise success.

6. **Consider relaxation techniques.** Mediation, biofeedback and controlled breathing can all help you relax and redirect negative thoughts.

7. **Be your best self.** You don't need to pretend to be anyone else. Your audience is here to hear your insights. Be your best self, act natural, smile and make eye contact.

8. **Worst case scenario, perhaps there is some underlying medical condition such as anxiety.** This is totally possible and in this case, you could need specialised help. If this is you it could be worth speaking to your doctor.

"If you don't know your audience, you won't be able to connect with them. And connection is vital when you want to convey a message through your speaking.

Not knowing your content

Not knowing your content well prior to delivering it can put you on the back foot in your presentation. And simply memorising it can lead to a robotic delivery that is boring. In both cases, when it comes time to deliver, performance stress can cause you to falter even when you might otherwise know the information.

Solutions to not knowing your content

To combat the risk of derailment on stage, you will need to know your content cold. This means that you need to go beyond simply practising and memorising, and move into rehearsing and knowing. You will not just need to memorise your speech, but know it backwards and forwards while also considering questions the audience may ask (and know your responses to those questions backwards and forwards too).

Remember that you should also consider not just your words, but also your actions and transitions between points to emphasise your message. Start by creating a space that mimics where you'll be delivering so that you can rehearse well. Move the furniture out of your office, stand up out of the chair and move around the room as if it were the stage. Rehearse where you'll walk, stand, and move between elements of your speech. And consider how you'll respond in different scenarios and to different audience responses. You'll want to ensure a single fluid delivery that becomes akin to muscle memory.

Getting to this point allows you to focus on your audience, rather than on your words, and gives you the time to adjust, respond or improvise during your speech itself.

Not knowing your audience

If you don't know your audience, you won't be able to connect with them. And connection is vital when you want to convey a message through your speaking. Connection helps you to get your audience on side, helps them engage with you and helps you to deliver a successful presentation.

Knowing your audience helps you to understand what content they care about and what is relevant to them. And once you know what to say, you'll also understand how best to deliver it in terms of your voice, tone and physical positioning.

When you *don't* know your audience, you won't be able to make those connections. When you can't connect, you can't engage and a disengaged audience is not going to be open to your message or willing to buy from you. Unfortunately, 60% of brand-created content – including presentations, speeches and keynotes – fails to deliver impactful consumer engagement.[17]

Solutions to not knowing your audience

1. **Do your homework.** Before you deliver any presentation or speech, find out as much as you can about your audience. This is broad information such as how many people will be in the audience, the shape and layout of the room and the general industries being represented. But it also includes any specifics you can find out, such as their roles at work, industry challenges or even their family situations.

---

17 Vizard, S. (1 February 2017). '60% of content created by brands is 'just clutter'.' Marketing Week. Accessed at https://www.marketingweek.com/content-havas-meaningful-brands/.

2. **Reach out.** Whatever you can't find out via research, you can discover by simply reaching out. Call people that fit the demographics of those you'll be speaking to (if you don't know precisely who will be in the audience). Ask about their problems and find out the specific situations they're facing.

3. **Get face-to-face.** If you have the opportunity, meet and greet people in your audience before you begin your presentation. You'll be able to find out a little bit about them. A friendly smile and a brief informal chat can go a long way to building fantastic engagement.

4. **Focus on your audience.** This is often the answer to many of the problems that hold us back from impactful presentations, but focusing on your audience is a great way to get to know them. You will need to be an authoritative expert, but always ensure that you're considering what your audience wants (and needs) rather than what you want.

5. **Take a birds-eye view.** When you're presenting to an audience, imagine that you're coming in above them, taking in everything that's happening in the room. What's the energy like? The vibe? What else is going on or happening at the conference or workshop? Who is speaking before you – or after?

All of these things will impact your audience, and, in turn, impact your delivery. For instance, if the CEO has just announced layoffs, this will impact how you deliver your speech to your audience. Similarly, news of a company expansion will impact your delivery in another way. An exceptional speaker understands all this and takes it all into account for every presentation they deliver.

Lack of energy or enthusiasm

When you're giving a speech, presentation or keynote, you need energy and a certain level of enthusiasm. This is the verbal and non-verbal 'oomph' that helps you deliver on stage.

Energy and enthusiasm can be shown in many different ways. Examples include your volume, your intonation, your smile and other facial expressions, the timing of your delivery and any special something that comes out during your performance. When you have energy as a speaker you are yourself but amplified. Your messaging has greater reach, but more importantly, your enthusiasm creates engagement and interest in what you're speaking about. After all, no one wants to listen to a boring presentation.

If you're lacking energy or enthusiasm, you'll likely struggle to engage and keep the interest of your audience. Without energy, you can come across as dull, dim, boring or even (in the worst cases) off-putting. Most importantly, you may face the serious risk of losing credibility. Nonverbal communication will speak louder than words every time.[18]

Solutions to a lack of energy or enthusiasm

To combat a lack of energy or enthusiasm, start by checking your posture. How you hold yourself and stand on stage matters. It not only impacts the amount of energy you have, but also the amount of oxygen that you can take in (which further impacts your energy).

---

18 Morgan, N. (November 2008). 'How to Become an Authentic Speaker.' *Harvard Business Review.* Accessed at https://hbr.org/2008/11/how-to-become-an-authentic-speaker.

When you
have energy
as a speaker you are
yourself but amplified.
Your messaging has greater
reach, but more importantly,
your enthusiasm creates
engagement and interest
in what you're
speaking about.

You also need to take ownership of your topic. Believe in yourself, believe in your subject matter and believe that you have something to offer. Allow that passion to shine through. This will give you more energy. Your state on stage is everything so you need to find ways to get yourself into the right state. I personally put my headphones on and listen to songs I find really get my energy up and help me feel like we're going to have a great time!

Taking the time to connect with audience members beforehand, during a break or at the door as people come into the room can also really help to lift you. Our job is to change the room so we have to be high vibing, much more than the room is!

An ineffective physical presence

When you don't have a strong physical presence this can impact your ability to deliver a strong performance and create buy-in for your messaging. It also ties directly into your energy levels. An ineffective physical presence can be due to many things, including lack of strong eye contact, fidgeting with hair (or genitals), touching your face or adjusting your clothing, speaking with a weak voice and even not using the stage fully.

This last element – not using the stage fully – can sometimes be difficult to nail down. When you stand in one place during your speech, or worse, at the back of the stage or in a far corner, you can come across as diffident and people may doubt your expertise.

Solutions to an ineffective physical presence

The solutions here depend on what is causing your on-stage problems. If you're struggling with fidgeting, first try to eliminate the cause of the problem. If you struggle with readjusting your clothes, find something more comfortable to wear. If you are constantly touching your hair, then pull it back. On the other hand, if you're touching your face a lot, hold something in your hands. It could be something small, like a pen, or a 'prop' relevant to your speech.

Then incorporate appropriate movements. The work of Dr Louise Mahler in the areas of body language and the use of gestures as learned from the ancient Greeks and Romans is extremely insightful here. In her book, *Gravitas: Timeless Skills to Communicate with Confidence and Build Trust,* she teaches us that body work – particularly gestures – played a vital part in the study of oration in ancient times.[19] Though we've had a fear of gestures – with conventional wisdom telling us they are distracting and unprofessional when speaking – when we use gestures well on stage, we can build confidence and influence with our audience.

When it comes to learning how to own the stage, look at some great speakers. Watch how they move around the space, how they engage with their audience by using the stage to their advantage. You'll also see how they're able to make eye contact (which can be a struggle with stage lighting).

---

19 Mahler, L. (2024). *Gravitas: Timeless Skills to Communicate with Confidence and Trust.* Wiley.

Dry mouth

A common problem that many speakers face is dry mouth[20], especially when feeling anxious or nervous. This is a problem that I have as well.

Experiencing a dry mouth can make it very difficult to perform the physical act of speaking. Your audience won't necessarily be aware that you're struggling with a physical problem and will more likely see it as evidence that you aren't prepared, or confident, in your message.

Solutions to dry mouth

Interestingly, there is a quick way to combat dry mouth. If you're experiencing this on the stage, quickly press your tongue against the roof of your mouth as hard as you can. This act stimulates the salivary glands which will combat dry mouth. You'll then be able to speak clearly and with confidence.

Not focusing on the business of speaking

Mastering content, connection and delivery is vital, but many speakers make the costly mistake of overlooking the business side of speaking – and this can certainly hold you back from being an exceptional speaker. To thrive as a speaker, you must see every gig not just as a performance, but as a business as well. Focusing only on what happens on the stage, and neglecting the practical aspects of managing the before and after, the relationships, the marketing and positioning and even your team's workflow, can lead to lost opportunities, lumpy income and unnecessary stress.

---

20 Dry mouth – Illnesses & conditions. (13 December 2022). NHS Inform. Accessed on nhsinform.scot/illnesses-and-conditions/mouth/dry-mouth.

"
To
thrive as a
speaker, you must
see every gig not just as
a performance. Treat your
speaking as a business, so you
can build a sustainable career
and make sure that every
opportunity on stage leads
to something
bigger.
"

Solutions to the business side of speaking

To truly reach Rockstar status, you must elevate both your performance and your business practice. Treat your speaking as a business, so you can build a sustainable career and make sure that every opportunity on stage leads to something bigger.

Follow our tips in Exceptional Commerciality, Chapter 6 and you'll be on the road to building an excellent speaking business!

When things go wrong

Sometimes things go wrong when you're presenting. Once I was speaking at a big conference in a major resort on the Gold Coast. The venue was like a nightclub. There were lights, and music and everyone was absolutely pumped. About a thousand people were attending, everyone was pouring in and the emcee was arriving. When it was almost time for me to speak on stage, I introduced myself to the AV guy and noticed that the presentation he had on his screen looked a bit different to the one that I had supplied.

He let me have a quick look and I saw that some slides were missing, and some contained new content that I had never seen before. I started to panic. I had prepared and rehearsed carefully, and with the correct slides.

But what could I do? It was too late to change the slides and certainly too late to pull out (which I wouldn't have done). So I took a deep breath and went looking for a whiteboard. I pulled it on stage, they mic'd me up and gave me the remote to click through the slides. They then told me I could only click my slides forward and couldn't go backwards.

I got up on stage and started my presentation. As I often do, I started with a story. Then I noticed my slides were moving automatically without me even touching the remote. The audience was looking at the slides, and the content didn't match what I was saying. So, in front of everyone, I had to ask the AV guy if he could please start the slides again. He did, but sure enough, they started moving on their own again before I was ready.

So I decided to stop and just turn the slides off.

It was a 45-minute keynote, and I went right through it to the end without any slides or tech at all. When I got off stage I thought, 'Oh they're not going to be happy. I don't know if I'm going to be asked back.' But the coordinator came running up to me, and said, 'That was amazing. I have no idea how you did that. We're definitely getting you back next year. And just so you know, your remote was connected to the room next door, and theirs was connected to yours!'

My experience shows that anything can happen when you're speaking on stage. Things come up and you need to know how to manage them. It was a good lesson learned for me.

When you're preparing for a presentation you need to understand that anything can happen. Because if you're not prepared for anything then it can really throw you off your game. Of course, there's no way to be prepared for everything that could possibly happen. It's more about having the mindset that things might not go precisely to plan, and a belief that it can still work out anyway.

Consider what you'll do if things don't go to plan. What if the mic stops working? What if your slides don't work? What visual aids will you use to help you if technology doesn't work?

I like to map up a timeline of my presentation on an A4 piece of paper so I know where I'm going if things go wrong.

Max Walker, one of the greatest orators shared the map of his last keynote at a Professional Speakers Association conference just before he passed away.

I have watched great speakers like Seth Godin and Dr Jason Fox speak who also use these mud maps on stage and don't use any slides for their speaking.

You are a professional and being paid the big bucks, so you need to know what to do and how to take the lead when things go wrong.

Conclusion

Becoming an exceptional speaker means doing the work. Keeping these techniques and ideas in mind as you prepare your presentations is a great first step, as well as being mindful of what might hold you back.

Understanding these things, and putting these techniques into practise will help you get closer to achieving your 'Rockstar' status, positioning you to make real impact and achieve real change.

CHAPTER 3

EXCEPTIONAL CONTENT

'There are three things to aim at in public speaking: first, to get into your subject, then to get your subject into yourself, and lastly, to get your subject into the heart of your audience.'

— Alexander Gregg

In Chapters 1 and 2 we covered the broad strokes of exceptional speaking and impactful presentations, including what they are and why they matter. But now it's time to get into the nitty-gritty. And that starts with how to create the exceptional content you need for a presentation that truly has impact.

Narrowing down your presentation content naturally involves several steps. However, the first step is understanding your message. You have to be clear in your own message from the start before you can deliver it to anyone else, particularly if you want to deliver it with impact.

How to get started understanding your message

When I'm giving speaking training, I'll often ask my clients what their key message is. In fact, I'll ask them to narrow it down to a single word. It's incredible how often people are unsure of that single word or find it difficult to narrow down their message. But finding your one-word message is really helpful, because it's from here that you gain the clarity to extrapolate the rest of your message in a concise and impactful way.

Finding your message

Finding your one-word message isn't always easy. To begin, ask yourself, 'What is the one thing you'd like your audience to take away? What is the single thing that you want them thinking, feeling or doing?' After all, what you really want your audience to go away saying is, 'I remember her presentation. It was about *this*.' That is your one-word message.

To get started narrowing down your message, consider the main theme that runs throughout your presentation. US motivational speaker Dave Carey was a prisoner of war in the infamous Ha Lò Prison, also known as the 'Hanoi Hilton', in Vietnam. Today he shares those experiences to inspire audiences and help organisations with team building and organisational development.

When Dave discusses how he delivers such incredibly impactful presentations, he focuses on the importance of having a theme, describing it as a memory aid. A strong theme provides a thread of continuity for your message that ensures you stay on topic and deliver a speech that makes sense to the audience.

I often think about a theme as an anchor. Throughout your presentation when you feel like you're going off course, your anchor – your one-word theme – will pull you back. Even better, it keeps you on point which, in turn, keeps your audience engaged.

Joe McCormack, who wrote the book *Brief,* found in his research that the average person can absorb 650 words per minute but can only speak 150 words per minute.[21] That's quite a gap! As speakers we need to bridge the gap between the amount that we're able to speak (not much) and the amount that the audience can perceive (much more!).

Having a thread that runs through your presentation allows the audience to remain engaged when their minds (naturally) start to become distracted. Your theme anchors their experience which supports familiarity and helps them dip back into your presentation easily if their attention drifts.

Your one word might be as simple as 'exceptional' (which could be the one-word theme of this book). Or it could be 'impact' or 'space' or 'balance' or even 'reach'. Whatever it is that your presentation centres around should become your one-word theme.

---

21 McCormack, J. (2014). *Brief: Make a Bigger Impact by Saying Less.* Wiley.

> You have to be clear in your own message from the start before you can deliver it to anyone else, particularly if you want to deliver it with impact.

Finding your bumper sticker

Once you find your one-word message, your next step is to expand on it. You can think of this expansion as your tagline or even like your presentation bumper sticker. If you were to stick your message on the back of your car, what would it say?

For example, it might be, 'Innovate to Succeed' or, 'Stand Out From the Crowd'. Or it might even be 'Creating Impactful Change'. Whatever it is, this three-, four- or five-word tagline is the next step to preparing your impactful content.

Your bumper sticker phrase should stand alone and represent the theme of your presentation without any further explanation. Of course, this won't be enough to deliver your message. But it should be enough to communicate the core essence of your presentation. In other words, it is the soul of your speech. Where your one word *focuses* your message, your bumper sticker *expands* that message. It will also help keep your audience engaged and bring them along with you during the journey of your presentation.

To find your presentation bumper sticker, think about what encapsulates the essence of your message. It needs to be a succinct phrase that conveys its fundamental nature. It must also establish value and communicate the benefit to your audience. The best bumper stickers are always audience-centric.

Getting this right is important. Impactful bumper stickers lead to impactful content which leads to impactful messages.

Finding your three core points

Once you've found your one-word message and your bumper sticker, then you can move on to finding your three core points. Just like your one-word message anchors your theme, your three core points provide the anchors for the structure and flow of your message, helping you move from one supporting element to the next.

Your three core points are also a memory aid for you because they allow you to identify the essence of your message, and make it easier to remember. Many experts agree that this helps them to memorise their speech because they can tackle each core point and their corresponding sections in turn.[22] Then it's a simple matter of pulling it all together.

In addition, there's a reason why the 'rule of three' is standard in the art of presentations.[23] The rule of three essentially says that you should present three or less key points to your audience in every speech or presentation. This is because people generally don't absorb or take away more than three points. It's best to keep your message very simple. And the rule of three helps you do just that.

A typical 45-minute keynote should have three main points. Each point will more often than not take five to seven minutes to unpack. When building out your three core points, think about some of the ways the rule of three has been used in the past – in media, in comms and in literature. One example is Winston Churchill's famous 'Blood, Sweat, and

22 Nawaz, S. (7 February 2020). 'Don't Just Memorize Your Next Presentation – Know It Cold.' *Harvard Business Review.* Accessed at https://hbr.org/2020/02/dont-just-memorize-your-next-presentation-know-it-cold.
23 Gallo. C. (2 July 2012). 'Thomas Jefferson, Steve Jobs, and the Rule of 3.' *Forbes.* Accessed at https://www.forbes.com/sites/carminegallo/2012/07/02/thomas-jefferson-steve-jobs-and-the-rule-of-3/?sh=72cf45621962.

To find your presentation bumper sticker, think about what encapsulates the essence of your message. It needs to be a succinct phrase that conveys its fundamental nature.

Tears' speech.[24] Other examples are the well-known films, *The Good, the Bad, and the Ugly* and *Sex, Lies, and Videotape*. These show how putting your message into a list of three helps it to be remembered.

When it comes to your own presentation you need to think about the three main points that you want your audience to remember. For example, if your presentation is about being prepared, then the three key points that sit under that might be:

1. First, know your outcome.

2. Second, do your homework.

3. Third, get ready for obstacles.

So, if you're delivering a presentation on health and wellbeing, the three points might be: eat healthily, exercise and enjoy life.

Of course, there are situations where you might want to move beyond the rule of three. If you only have a 20-minute presentation, you might only have time for two main points. If you have a 60-minute presentation, you might have time for four or even possibly five. But in those cases, you'll still want to keep it very simple, clear and aligned to your one-word message.

Robert Cialdini wrote the book *Influence: A Psychology Of Persuasion*.[25] In it he says that when we can loop our message back to our key areas (or core points), we're able to change people's perceptions and influence their actions. I would encourage you in your next presentation to ensure you are clear on your core points and that you are continually

---

24 Rothman, L. (13 May 2015). 'This Is the Speech That Made Winston Churchill's Career.' *Time*. Accessed at https://time.com/3848735/churchill-best-speeches-blood-toil-tears-sweat/.

25 Cialdini, R. (2006). *Influence: The Psychology of Persuasion*. Harper Business.

looping your message back to them. In this way you'll be able to change people's minds and influence their actions too.

Audience analysis

Understanding what you want to say is the first step. Now that you understand your message, you need to stop and think about your audience. How is your message going to be received by your audience? Understanding your audience is going to impact your content as you flesh it out.

Why does this matter? Because if you're not very clear about who you're speaking to, your presentation is not going to be relatable to them. You need to understand who your audience is and, importantly, what their challenges and fears are. I often say that the person who understands the customer and the audience best is the person who wins.

Ken Haemer, former AT&T's Manager of Presentation Design, said that designing a presentation without an audience in mind is like writing a love letter and addressing it 'to whom it may concern'. Any recipient of that love letter certainly wouldn't feel the love was meant for them, and they wouldn't be engaged with the sender.

In the same way, a generic presentation will make your audience feel disengaged. It will make them feel like you don't understand them and aren't interested in their world.

Understand your audience's *why*

In Matt Church's book, *Amplifiers*, he says that we don't spend enough time on *why*.[26] 'Why' *is* about purpose – of course – but it's about more than that. It's also about giving you a framework to develop a presentation that has purpose *and* impact. By understanding your audience, you will be able to unpack and articulate why what you're saying is important to them. And that is the crux of an impactful presentation.

Simon Sinek, who delivered the TED talk, 'Start With Why', believes that you need to take it a step further and think about *why should they care*?[27] When it comes to your audience, why should they care about what you have to say? Why should they care about *your* message in particular?

What this comes down to is understanding the challenges and fears of your audience. But to do this you really need to put yourself in their shoes.

If you're talking to managers, they may experience frustration as they struggle to motivate their team. They may feel they don't have a lot of time, or feel that they're spread pretty thin. They may wish people would do their job, or resent the time they have to spend giving feedback to team members who aren't toeing the line.

Or perhaps your audience is composed of executives. Perhaps they're struggling under budget pressures or pressures that come from leading

---

26 Church, M. (2020). *Amplifiers: The power of motivational leadership to inspire and influence.* Matt Church Pty Ltd.
27 Sinek, S. (29 September 2009). 'Start with why – how great leaders inspire action.' TEDxPugetSound. Accessed at https://www.youtube.com/watch?v=u4ZoJKF_VuA.

a nationwide organisation. Maybe they fear they lack gravitas, or are unable to directly reach all the employees within their large organisation.

If your audience is made up of small business owners their problems might be cashflow – they may not have the money to pay wages for the next two weeks. Maybe they're feeling that they've been spread very thin, having to keep up the work of the business as well as the unseen work of marketing, accounting, staff recruitment and training. Often small business owners don't have any support crew or an IT department. They're it, and their fear is having to go back to a job full time.

If your audience is women in business, their challenge could be that they're juggling it all. They might have children in school or daycare. They might be struggling to find the time to look after themselves. Their fear is not being able to manage it all. They also fear that they're not going to succeed – that they're going to fail.

Whoever your audience is, they will have distinct and unique fears and problems. You need to ask yourself, 'What does this audience want you to understand about them?' The only way to do that is to understand what they're going through and amplify what's going on in their world. You really need to show your audience that you understand their problems and fears. Addressing these – whether obliquely or outright – is a recipe for creating impact in your content.

But how do you get that information? How do you find out what your audience's fears and problems are?

Finding the challenges & fears

When you begin to prepare for a presentation, I suggest that you spend some time identifying your audience and understanding the challenges and fears they face. To get that information, you simply need to go out and find it. You should start by interviewing an audience member. Someone that will actually be in the audience when you deliver your presentation. Then you simply ask them what their problems or challenges are and what their fears are.

Of course, many people don't want to acknowledge their challenges and fears. If the person you're speaking to is reluctant to open up, think of how you can connect with them to get the information you need. Perhaps phrase your questions with lead-ins such as, 'in your industry' or 'amongst your competitors'. You might say, 'Amongst your competitors what do you see as the greatest challenge day to day?'

Let's say, for example, that I am going to speak to a group of early career female lawyers I haven't spoken to before. To get inside the mind of this particular audience I might find out who is going to attend the event and then go and pay for one lawyer's time. It's well worth it for me to pay a small amount for an hour-long interview with them so that I can find out and understand the challenges and fears faced by members of the legal profession.

If you put some time and resources into finding out information about your audience before you begin preparing your presentation, you'll be able to build a relevant presentation that resonates with your audience. Identifying these problems will help you to tailor your speech or presentation. And as you tailor it to your audience you'll build more engagement and lasting impact.

"Your purpose statement isn't something you share with your audience. You use it to guide the research, organisation and writing of your content."

Your purpose statement

I suggest that you begin your audience analysis by composing an audience-centred purpose statement. This purpose statement is one sentence that lays out the objective of your speech from the perspective of your audience. For it to be impactful it must be aligned with your one-word theme and bumper sticker and contain the elements of your core points.

Your purpose statement isn't something you share with your audience. You use it to guide the research, organisation and writing of your content. It helps you to keep the perspective of your audience at the front of your mind throughout the content creation process.

Your purpose statement usually contains an explicit reference to your audience and should always be realistic. After all, you won't be able to teach an audience all the elements of content marketing (for example) in a 30-minute presentation. But you will be able to give them three core points to help them with their own challenges and problems.

So, what is a good purpose statement? Here's an example:

'After my presentation, my audience of managers will understand the effect of conscious leadership to recruit and retain talent, ease the pressures of team management and create space for creativity and innovation.'

As you can see, this statement is focused on the audience (managers), names the main theme (conscious leadership) and touches on three core points (talent, team management and creativity and innovation).

If you're wondering if you've crafted your purpose statement correctly, share it with someone who will be in the audience (or who would fit the audience profile). Get their feedback to see if it's hitting the mark. If it's not, make changes until it does.

Other audience elements

When you're completing your audience analysis, be sure to consider demographics other than just the role your audience members have at work. Other relevant elements could be:

- **Socio-demographic characteristics.** These include sex, gender, age, culture, economic situation and language.

- **Geographic characteristics.** This is where the audience lives and works and understanding this will give insight into their likely behaviour.

- **Psychographic characteristics.** These are the needs, concerns, challenges, hopes and aspirations of your target audience.

- **Societal characteristics.** Consider the beliefs, knowledge and actions that relate to social issues and the society in which the audience operates.

- **Educational characteristics.** What knowledge, information and skills does the audience possess and how can you utilise these in your presentation?

- **Communication characteristics.** How does your audience prefer to communicate and how can you use these channels to create engagement in your presentation?

- **Barriers to engagement.** What things might prevent your audience from accepting your message and taking action? How can you address these?

Creating your outline

Now that you've completed your preparatory work, you're ready to begin creating your content. And the first important step is creating your outline.

Your outline is a blueprint for your presentation. I know some presenters who don't bother with this, and if it doesn't work for you, that's OK. But for most speakers, it helps to first create the essential structure of your speech.

When you create your outline, start with your theme. Next comes your introduction, a body and a conclusion. Each of your core points makes up a different body section of your speech. Within those sections are the factors that will logically support your core message. You will also need to include the high-level concepts that you want to impart, including data and information, and the stories, metaphors and quotes that you want to use to communicate the core message.

Between each of your sections you will need to work out your transitions. How can you smoothly lead your audience between the core points of your presentation in a way that makes sense and feels logical to them? How can you tie everything together in a meaningful and audience-centric way? Your outline gives you the space to work this out.

Finally, you'll want to include rough timings for each part of your presentation. This ensures that you're spending enough time on the right elements of your message and aren't distracted by other parts that may be less important. It also ensures that you stay within your designated time limit.

High Impact Speaking Timeline

© Jane Anderson

1. Introduction [Time: 3 minutes]

   a. Story - your story introduces your concept and hooks the audience

   b. Problems - these are problems that the audience will face, and what you're hoping to solve with your big idea

   c. Master message - this is the big idea that you want your audience to walk away with

   d. Analogy - an analogy or metaphor that explains your master message

   e. Transition

2. Body

    a. Core Point 1 [Time: 8 minutes]

        i. Supporting elements, including information, data, stories, metaphors and quotes

        ii. Transition

    b. Core Point 2 [Time: 8 minutes]

        i. Supporting elements, including information, data, stories, metaphors and quotes

        ii. Transition

    c. Core Point 3 [Time: 8 minutes]

        i. Supporting elements, including information, data, stories, metaphors and quotes

        ii. Transition

3. Conclusion [Time: 3 minutes]

    a. Recap points - briefly go through your three core points

    b. Prescription - here you give your solution, but don't give away all your IP as you want them to come and work with you

    c. Q&A - allow time for questions and answers and have a system in place to take those questions

    d. Quote - an authoritative quote underscores what you've done in the room and on the stage

The importance of stories

One thing to touch on is the importance of stories in your content. Stories help you to bring your message to life. They keep your audience engaged and help them to remember the more mundane elements that they might otherwise forget. That's because stories help form a personal connection to your message, making it stick. Long after your speech is done, your audience will remember the interesting stories that you told.

Research shows that storytelling is a powerful tool for catalysing change.[28] It allows complex ideas to be shared in a meaningful and easy-to-digest way. It helps people to focus on new ideas and novel concepts in a way that feels nonthreatening. And sharing stories allows you to build rapport and therefore trust with your audience.

When you share powerful, memorable or meaningful stories, you build connections with your audience, and you create both emotional impact and capacity for creative and innovative thinking. This creates a space for your message to land and be retained.

When you're preparing your content, be sure to consider the stories that will best illustrate your message and help to embed it in your listeners' minds. These can be humorous, emotional, uplifting or even sad or traumatic, as long as they contribute to furthering your message and engaging with your audience.

---

28 Denning, S. (2002). 'How storytelling ignites action in knowledge-era organisations.' *The Journal of Perinatal Education*. Accessed at https://www.ncbi. nlm.nih.gov/pmc/articles/PMC1595111/.

"
When you share
powerful, memorable
or meaningful stories, you
build connections with your
audience, and you create
both emotional impact
and capacity.
"

Crafting your exceptional content

The final step in crafting your presentation content is to flesh out everything that you will ultimately deliver. However, with all the preparatory work you've done, this step will likely take much less time than you might think.

Review your full outline and begin writing out what you're going to say for each part – the introduction, each of the body sections highlighting your core points, all the stories you'll include and the transitions between each section. Remember to always keep your audience in mind – ensuring you stay focused on communicating to that particular group of people. Always be mindful of their biggest problems and fears to ensure you understand and are providing solutions and adding value. This will allow you to create the content you need in order to have the impact you want.

A highly recommended approach is to use the content pages process discussed in my book, *Catalyst Content*. This process helps you to create thought leadership assets for your keynote that can also be used to leverage your expertise into income streams for your growth.

Conclusion

At the end of the day your content is simply your message. In preparing your presentation content, you're really just searching for the best way to deliver it to your particular audience. Anyone can put together an outline of information. But it's only by really understanding your message and thoroughly diving into your audience, understanding their fears, challenges, problems, goals and needs, that you can get there!

CHAPTER 4

EXCEPTIONAL CONNECTION

'The success of your presentation will be judged not by the knowledge you send but by what the listener receives.'

— Lilly Walters

Now that we've discussed how to create exceptional content, we need to talk about how to deliver that content. And delivering exceptional content comes down to one fundamental thing – exceptional connection.

Why does connection matter?

One of the most important aspects of public speaking is connecting with your audience. This is the ability to engage your audience, to bring them into the conversation and even into the world you are creating during your presentation. Importantly, connection with your audience allows you to understand their reactions, wants and needs. And that means you can deliver more of what they are looking for while presenting, which further deepens your engagement and creates greater impact for your message.

Of course, that might be easier said than done. After all, how do we create connection, let alone exceptional connection? What exactly do we need to do to create engagement and impact? Most importantly, how do we create exceptional connection in our presentations?

Choosing connection over perfection

To truly connect with your audience, you need to embrace what is truly, authentically you. And that means throwing out any notion of perfection. While you'll hear me wax lyrical about the importance of knowing your content and rehearsing your delivery, the purpose is to step outside yourself and get into the minds of your audience. But rehearsing should not be confused with demanding perfection.

There has never been – and never will be – a perfect presentation. So take the pressure off yourself by not aiming for perfection.

Craig Valentine, 1999 World Champion of Public Speaking, advises us to focus on connection, not perfection.[29] This piece of advice helps you to stop looking inward and instead enables you to turn your attention outward. And when you can do that, it allows more of your individuality and authenticity to shine through. You will be more relatable, and your audience will be more empathetic to you and more amenable to your message.

In fact, if someone comes across as too perfect, they can almost seem robotic or like an automaton. As much as we might claim to like perfection, the truth is that most people don't. Employers are more likely to hire someone that owns up to their weaknesses than someone who humblebrags about their 'perfectionism', for example.[30] It's the little glimpses of imperfection that make us likeable, sympathetic and approachable.

Embracing your authentic best

A huge part of connection is embracing not just your authenticity but your authentic best self and conveying that to your audience. And to do that you need to bring the essence of you into your presentation.

When you bring your authentic best self into your presentation, you are conveying more than your words can impart. American essayist, lecturer and philosopher Ralph Waldo Emerson said, 'Who you are

29 (8 January 2013). '1999 Toastmasters World Champion of Public Speaking Craig Valentine Shares His Insights.' Speaking Sherpa. Accessed at https://speakingsherpa.com/1999-toastmasters-world-champion-of-public-speaking-craig-valentine-shares-his-insights/.
30 Lebowitz, S. (14 March 2019). '14 things you're doing that make people instantly dislike you.' Business Insider. Accessed at https://www.businessinsider.com/things-that-make-people-dislike-you-2017-3.

> By bringing the essence of you and your personal brand into your presentation, you can create a great connection with the audience that lets you push through any lingering distance (and any brick walls).

speaks so loudly I can't hear what you're saying.' Of course, you don't want to drown out your message with your personality. But conversely, if you don't embrace your personality, no one will hear your message.

When you are delivering a presentation without embracing your authentic personality, you can think of it like putting up a brick wall. Your lack of authenticity creates a block between you and your audience, stopping them from hearing you, seeing you and, importantly, connecting with you.

As the presenter you want to do as much as you can to remove that wall. Your personality is what will enable your message to connect. By bringing the essence of you and your personal brand into your presentation, you can create a great connection with the audience that lets you push through any lingering distance (and any brick walls).

Using humour for authenticity

I worked with a senior researcher at the University of the Philippines who excelled at bringing his personality into his presentations. He was an Indian gentleman working in finance with an oil and gas company. He had quite a strong accent for Australian audiences, and this might seem like it could have created difficulties in hearing his message. But in fact, it became a strength of his presentation.

He often told stories about growing up in India with his family, humorously recounting stories from his childhood. He was likeable, funny, entertaining, happy and easy to listen to. His accent and background were the platform for him to bring his authentic self into his presentation. And his audience found it easy to engage with him because of it.

Finding your own path to exceptional connection

You will have your own unique elements that you can use to create connection with your audience. And many of these you might not even realise you have. But everyone – without exception – has something.

Perhaps you have a physical element to showcase (you might be very tall or skilled at a sport or hobby). Perhaps you have lived in many different countries or learned several languages. Or maybe you are very gregarious. Whatever is unique to you, you can bring onto the stage. Your unique essence can help you share your energy and personality and form connections through your presentation and presentation collateral.

Morgan Spurlock, gave a TED talk called, 'The greatest TED Talk ever sold', and in it he interviewed people about their personal brands. He asked them what made them unique. Each had their own angle. One was part hippie, part yogi. Another was a 'lawyer' brand. And another had the catchphrase, 'Ugly but honest'.

Whatever it is, if you can create authentic characterisation and differentiate yourself from the thousands of other run-of-the-mill presenters who get on stage, that will work to your advantage. I would encourage you to really think about what is authentically you. Because it's this authenticity that will create the connection.

For myself, I have brought certain unique elements into my own personal brand. For example, I grew up in a regional area in Northern New South Wales where there was a big hippie culture. Because of this, my personal brand also incorporates a little bit of the Australian country and a little bit of the hippie culture.

Both of these are a part of my character and part of my own unique personality that I bring to the stage when I need to. When I bring these elements to the stage, I'm able to create different energy levels, differentiate my presentation from others and help the audience connect with me.

If you're looking for the unique elements of your own personal brand, ask yourself these questions:

1. How would you describe your personal brand? What words come to mind – funny, gentle, assertive?

2. Where are you from? Did you grow up in a different country, in a country town, by the coast, in a busy urban environment or in the middle of nowhere?

3. What are your standout qualities? Are you a super organised perfectionist or more creative and chaotic? How can you embrace those qualities?

Remember that even so-called 'negative' elements – such as saying 'I'm boring or middle-aged or pedantic' – can be a fantastic way to build connection. For example, I worked with one speaker, an accountant, who used to bring into his presentations how pedantic he was about planning his speaking trips. But because he was funny and self-deprecating, and a lot of people could relate to his process, it was an excellent way to build connection with his audience.

Preparation

Once you understand the elements that you're planning on using to create exceptional connection, it's important to deliver those elements in the best way you can. And exceptional connection involves preparation.

The first way that you can prepare to connect is by learning how to manage yourself physically. This starts with your heart rate. To manage your heart rate, you can use apps to help you breathe in six-second cycles. They can help to decrease stress and improve your focus[31] – both vital elements to creating connection and impactful presentations.

Self-care is very important when talking about connection. If you don't feel your best, you simply won't be able to put your best self out into the world. And people in your audience will be able to pick up on that energy or vibe.

To prepare to put your best self in front of your audience, start by getting enough sleep. If you don't have enough sleep your brain can't retain the information it needs and you won't have the energy you need.

Second, make sure that you're eating good foods that make you feel alert and focused. For me, and many speakers, it's important to have breakfast. You need blood sugar and glucose to be able to make sure your brain functions on the day.

Before you go on stage, be sure to take a bit of time to centre yourself. Turn everything off – your mobile phone, computer notifications and anything else that might interrupt you. Take yourself away somewhere quiet, where you can be alone. You might want to go on a walk or lock yourself away in a quiet room or even hide in a bathroom if you have to. Just go, get your own space for a few minutes and have some quiet moments to centre yourself so you can feel ready to share yourself with your audience.

---

31 Zaccaro, A, et al. (7 September 2018). 'How Breath-Control Can Change Your Life: A Systematic Review on Psycho-Physiological Correlates of Slow Breathing'. *Frontiers in Neuroscience*. Accessed at https://www.ncbi.nlm.nih.gov/pmc/articles/PMC6137615/.

"

Self-care is very important when talking about connection. If you don't feel your best, you simply won't be able to put your best self out into the world.

"

You also need to prepare for the unexpected, including how to manage the energy in the room. Once I delivered a presentation on the Gold Coast to a group of small business owners in the health and wellbeing industry. But what I failed to do is double check the agenda to see who was on stage before me and what they would be presenting.

I had prepared a high-energy presentation, but when I walked in the previous speakers were just starting their presentation, and I suddenly realised they were running a meditation. I couldn't follow this very calming presentation by coming in with the really loud 'Righteo, let's go.' I had to start where the audience was in terms of energy (which was low) and then build it up to match my presentation (which was high). This meant modifying how I interacted with the audience on the stage.

Finally, you'll want to prepare more than just the words you will say. When you're on stage, things like eye contact, pauses, hand gestures and body placement are all important to manage the energy in the room and create connection with your audience. As Mark Twain said, *'The right word may be effective, but no word was ever as effective as a rightly timed pause.'*

Storytelling

Aristotle was a student of Plato and studied at Plato's Academy from the time he was aged 18 all the way through the age of 37.[32] Many consider him to be the original scientist. But Aristotle was also a master communicator and laid the foundation for spoken communication that we still use today.

---

32 Aristotle (384 B.C.E.–322 B.C.E.). *Internet Encyclopedia of Philosophy.* Accessed at https://iep.utm.edu/aristotle/.

Aristotle said that spoken presentations need three elements. These are ethos (authority), logos (logic) and pathos (emotion).

Ethos

Ethos is authority. But how do you gain authority or credibility? You can certainly do this through your own thought leadership. And many experts will achieve this over time. However, you can also create credibility simply by citing experts or credible sources. Perhaps this is Steve Jobs or Bill Gates, if you're in the IT industry. Or if you're in the leadership space, perhaps it's Simon Sinek or Robin Sharma.

You can also focus on using scientific or scholarly research in your field. This will show that your ideas are well considered and well supported. And that will convey to your audience that you are credible and believable.

Logos

Logos is logic. And to meet this requirement you need to consider the evidence and data behind everything that you're talking about in your presentation.

Again, this might be met through scientific or scholarly research which can be used to provide the reasoning or the data behind your position. Or you can conduct your own primary research by polling your clients or a specific group of people to gain some insight and context.

Pathos

The last element is pathos, or emotional connection. There are many ways to create this emotional connection with your audience – but one of the best is through storytelling.

Joseph Campbell wrote the book, *The Hero with a Thousand Faces*, first published in 1949.[33] This book was a work of comparative mythology that analysed the typical structure of the hero's journey throughout the myths of the world.

The hero's journey has a regular structure. In the beginning there's a call to adventure which is followed by a crisis. The hero then receives some aid, sometimes supernatural and sometimes through a mentor, guardian or helper. Ultimately, the hero is successful in their quest and comes home changed or transformed.

Of course, there are often other elements included, particularly around the crisis. There might be a death or some abuse. But in the end, there's always a rebirth or renewal, an atonement and a return home. In all cases the journey is moving from the unknown to the known, or from the adventure to home.

Since Campbell's seminal work, the hero's journey has been used for many of the world's most popular films. One fantastic example of this is *Star Wars*, and we still have many movies being made according to this archetype today.

However, in the 1970s some movies started to deviate from the hero's journey archetype in a significant way – they didn't all have happy

---

33 Campbell, J. (1949). *Hero With A Thousand Faces*. Pantheon Press.

"

Using storytelling
in your speaking
is important, and
incorporating elements
of the hero's journey can
help you tap into that
emotional connection.

"

endings anymore. These films tended not to be financially successful, as they did not resonate with their audience.

Using storytelling in your speaking is important, and incorporating elements of the hero's journey can help you tap into that emotional connection. Storytelling creates what's called *soft power* and paves the path to the pathos element of Aristotle's principles. It really connects to the heart of your audience.

Gabrielle Dolan, in her co-authored book, *Hooked: How Leaders Connect, Engage and Inspire with Storytelling*,[34] tells the story of the National Australia Bank executive who was trying to get his team members to attend the regular Monday morning meeting. He was finding it quite frustrating and wondered why they just wouldn't come along. Instead, they would drag their feet and procrastinate. It took forever for everyone to get into the room.

Gabrielle asked him to recall a time when he had to get something over and done with. He remembered a childhood experience where his mom was trying to get him to eat Brussels sprouts. She would tell him just to eat the Brussels sprouts first so he could then go and enjoy the rest of his meal.

Gabrielle told the executive that this was exactly the story that he needed to tell. So at the next Monday morning meeting, he told that story. And then he compared the meeting to eating their Brussels sprouts, suggesting that if they could get through it quickly, they'd have the rest of the week to focus on other tasks. This story resonated with his team, and as a result, he was able to get them to their meeting.

---

34 Dolan, G & Naidu, Y. (2013). *Hooked: How Leaders Connect, Engage and Inspire with Storytelling*. Wiley.

Balancing out your storytelling

When it comes to storytelling, it's important to remember not to make all the stories about you. It's fine to include some, and that can actually be quite a connecting process. However, you have to make sure the balance is right. You'll have more impact if your stories are a balance of you and others.

Remember, it's not necessarily about having a *good* story, because there's no such thing. As Martin Conradi said in his book, *That Presentation Sensation*, stories are simply good or bad in the telling.[35]

So, how do you bring stories into your presentation? First, your stories should link to your values *and* your message (often this is easy because your message will likely link to a value that you hold). Second, if you're looking to get ideas, you might ask yourself some questions to get started.

I had a lovely woman called Janet come to one of my speaking courses because she needed to deliver a presentation on data entry for a new learning management system. She said to me, 'I have no idea how I'm going to make this interesting.'

One of the activities I had the entire group do was bring along one of their most prized possessions to the course. Janet brought along a photo of her feet. The story about the picture came out.

A few years ago, Janet and her best friend went on a bush walk to a beautiful waterfall. As they were walking down towards the waterfall, she slipped and became wedged, mostly submerged in the water. She tried

---

35 Conradi, M. (2001). *That Presentation Sensation: Be Good, Be Passionate, Be Memorable.* Financial Times Prentice Hall.

to get out, and her friend tried to help her, but her feet were completely stuck. Her friend tried to call for help, but they were out of range. Janet was stuck, and she was wet and very cold.

Her friend had to leave her there and race two hours back up the trail to get to a spot where she could call for help. When she called the helicopter, she had to give the exact coordinates of where she was so they could be found and her friend could be rescued.

This story became an integral part of her keynote presentation. She was able to link her story to why it's so important to have certain data entered in a learning management system. And that made her message really stick.

Don't be put off if you think your best stories won't work. Janet's story shows how a story that might at first not relate to your presentation can work very well as a metaphor or simply to engage the audience.

Other stories that you might use could be your favourite travel destination, your favourite hobby or activity outside of work, or it could also be your signature dish. For example, a participant in one of my recent training sessions had Pavlova as her signature dish. In a presentation to an oil and gas company, she talked about preparing it for Christmas last year and how much time it takes to get it right, despite being a fairly simple process with limited ingredients. However, she needed to take the time to get it right. When she didn't, she'd ruined the Pavlova and ended up losing time and having to start over.

Her message in her presentation was all about taking it slow and checking everything. She shared the message that if you put a little time into planning, you'll actually save time in the long run. The story about her Pavlova worked really well. It brought the speaker's essence into her presentation, but it was also light and funny and it delivered the message that she needed it to.

When it comes to building up your own storytelling suite, I would suggest keeping a journal of stories. I would also suggest when you're putting together your stories, use the hero's journey archetype but align it with the emotional challenges people in your audience may have.

Analogies

Another way to create connection with your audience is through analogies. Analogies have a lot of impact and can captivate an audience very quickly. They also quickly establish context for your message, particularly if you've got very technical information, which can be boring and difficult to succinctly convey to an audience.

There's a fantastic book called *I Never Metaphor I Didn't Like*, by Dr Mardy Grothe[36], that I always suggest to my community. It really brings attention to the power of metaphor and posits that it's one of the most versatile tools to express a strong idea.

As well as context, analogies in your presentations create contrast and a conduit between your message and the world your audience understands. Analogies work especially well for big-picture people, enabling them to make connections. And when they make those connections, then you've achieved impact.

You can think of an analogy as a bit like a compass. It gives your audience a direction, a path to your message – particularly when it's a bit complex

---

36 Grothe, M. (2008). *I Never Metaphor I Didn't Like: A Comprehensive Compilation of History's Greatest Analogies, Metaphors, and Similes.* HarperCollins US.

" You can think of an analogy as a bit like a compass. It gives your audience a direction, a path to your message – particularly when it's a bit complex or multi-faceted. "

or multi-faceted. An analogy can even be likened to a rescue team who can help lead your audience to 'safety' so they aren't lost along the way. The use of AI can be really helpful in finding metaphors much faster than ever before.

Using body language & gestures

When it comes to presenting, how you use your body on stage is vital to building a real connection with your audience. Let's refer back to Dr Louise Mahler's work on body language and gestures.[37] In her work studying ancient and modern body language techniques, she found that when we can develop these skills and use them well, we can build our impact and influence when we present – in other words, we can build our connection.

Dr Mahler's work showcases how aligning our verbal and nonverbal communication – and here we're referring to making our body and gestures on stage align with the message that we're delivering – can ensure we make the greatest impact and have the most effective delivery.

Unfortunately, many speakers have been taught from a very young age to avoid too many gestures. We've been taught that gestures will distract and undermine our overall message. So we try to be still, keeping our hands clenched and our arms tight against our bodies. And this lack of natural movement then impacts our ability to deliver authentically.

Instead, Dr Mahler shows us how looking to ancient orators and their study of the skills of delivery, including gestures can help us to be exceptional speakers. Her work gives us three golden rules of gestures:

_____

37 Mahler. Gravitas.

1. Non-repetitive

2. Congruent

3. Held[38]

So when we use gestures on stage, we need to ensure that we aren't making the same ones over and over again, that each gesture aligns with our words and is therefore congruent, and that we hold one gesture until we're ready to make the next one. When we do this we'll be in a great position to have more impact in our presentations, make better connections and become an exceptional speaker.

Rehearsing

It should go without saying, but one of the best ways to make an impact and really bring together all the above elements into your presentation is to rehearse. The more you rehearse your presentation, the more you'll be ready to deliver on the big day.

Natalie Cook and Kerri Pottharst, the Australian beach volleyballers who won gold at the 2000 Olympics in front of their home crowd in Byron Bay, didn't win just by showing up on the day. They achieved their gold medals only after years and years of practise and honing their individual and combined skills. In fact, when Natalie was interviewed courtside after the game, she was asked how it felt to win. She said, 'It's exactly how I remembered it!'

It's no different for presentations. There is a useful rule attributed to 18th-century American philosopher Wayne Burgraff. He said it takes one hour of preparation for each minute of your presentation time. I agree

---

38 Mahler. Gravitas.

with this. The more you prepare and practise, the better you will be and the more impact you will have.

Nowadays there are some great AI tools that will allow you to deliver your presentation and even give you feedback on how engaging you are by assessing things such as tone, questions and humour.

So, if you want to create exceptional connection, you must make sure you prepare and rehearse.

Cocktail tests

Part of rehearsing is testing, and one great way to do that is through cocktail tests. Cocktail tests are simply where you try out elements of your presentation in informal settings (aka, cocktail parties!). So you might tell an anecdote to your mates at the pub or share an analogy with your friends at lunch or over coffee.

A cocktail test is a great way to test your content, but don't tell people that you're doing it. Otherwise they're going to overanalyse it or even be too kind in their responses. The purpose of cocktail tests is to test your stories, particularly if you think they're funny, so you can see if people laugh or not and gauge their reactions.

The last thing you want to do is test something on stage live because it may just land flat. And when that happens, you lose the connection that you might have built with your audience. It's much better to discover that it's not going to work when your small group of friends don't laugh than to find out in front of a huge audience during your presentation.

Connection with event organisers

We wouldn't really be treating the idea of connection in speaking to its fullest without speaking about your connection with event organisers and those who are actually in charge of running the event. After all, these are the people who ultimately make your presentation – and therefore your speaking career – possible!

Your relationship with event organisers needs to begin long before you step on the stage and continue well after the presentation is over. And you need to put in the processes to support that relationship – and this comes down to exceptional connection.

So how can you build exceptional connection with event organisers?

- **Be easy to work with.** Exceptional connection means being responsive, reliable and adaptable to the needs of that individual (and the company or event they represent).

- **Think beyond the stage.** Keep in mind that connection doesn't end when you step off the stage. Exceptional speakers follow up, express gratitude and ask for feedback so they can improve.

- **Add value.** Adding value is one of the best ways to maintain strong connection. This might be in the form of videos, diagnostics, books or quizzes. You might also offer follow-up workshops or share tailored content that aligns with the organiser's needs.

- **Be bureau friendly.** If you're working with speakers bureaus, you must be bureau friendly. Maintain open communication, and be easy to recommend by being easy to work with, dependable and easy to represent.

- **Always debrief.** Book in your debrief session when you book the gig. This is a great opportunity to add value, get feedback and gently see whether any of your other offerings might be a good fit for the organiser and their organisation.

Conclusion

Building exceptional connection with your audience, as well as those booking the gigs, is a vital element to becoming an exceptional speaker and delivering an impactful presentation. Consider who you are, what your stories are and how to bring those elements into your speech. Think about what gestures and body language you can use that align with and elevate your overall message. Take care of yourself physically and mentally, and ensure that you rehearse and test, rehearse and test and rehearse and test again!

Once you've prepared, rehearsed and tested (and done it again and again) you will be in an excellent position to create the connections you need that will allow your audience to better understand and embrace the message you have to deliver.

CHAPTER 5

EXCEPTIONAL
COLLATERAL

'Images are the most powerful
communicator we have.'

— **John Berger, art critic, novelist, Booker Prize winner**

We've discussed our content and our connection, which we now understand are vital for delivering an exceptional speech or presentation. But now we need to really dive into the *visuals* of our presentation. Because the visuals are where we take our impact and really amplify it. And our visuals are part of our collateral.

What is your collateral?

Collateral is sometimes referred to as marketing collateral, and includes any branded asset that you use in your business to make it recognisable and memorable.

There are some standard collaterals that we all typically need. These include things like:

- Logo
- Icons
- Values and mission statement
- Website
- Bio
- Social profiles
- Business cards
- Brochures
- Newsletters and emails
- Blog posts
- E-books and books
- Guides and whitepapers
- Landing pages
- Testimonials and case studies
- Pitch deck
- Videos
- Animations
- Images
- Customer onboarding kits

- Thank you prompts
- Original graphics (graphs, charts, models)
- Podcast
- Reports, case studies and research projects
- Slides
- Diagnostics
- Branded community

But when it comes to our presentations, there are a few that we'll use more often than not. These are typically contained in our slides – the visual presentation that many people use when we're delivering on stage. In those slides, we may use things like:

- Logos
- Icons
- Original graphics (graphs, charts, models)
- Images
- Videos
- Animations
- Testimonials
- Case studies
- Bio

Each of these can help to elaborate on your message and engage the audience on multiple levels.

Other presentation collateral

Of course, we must also look beyond just our slides to the other collateral that's in or around the room before, during and after your presentation. This includes:

- **Your introduction:** Your intro is one of the most important parts of your presentation collateral because this is what the emcee says about you before you begin your presentation. It's important that you either write this yourself or read through the prepared introduction to ensure everything is accurate and sets you up to deliver in the best light. I've had some instances when my introductions have contained incorrect information – not a great start!

- **The table items provided for attendees:** While this may be more important when you're delivering a workshop, the items set out on the attendees' tables – pens, notebooks, business cards, etc – showcase who you are.

  For example, I always choose Blackwing pencils to put on the tables at my workshops simply because they are of exceptional quality and used by professional writers. By placing these on the table I'm demonstrating to my attendees that they can expect to have that elevated and exceptional experience.

- **Your banners:** These are the elements that hang behind you in the presentation room and that advertise your presentation outside of the room. Inside the room, you might choose banners that have your taglines or logos or that reiterate one or two main points of your message.

You don't want to have your images on the banners inside the room, as this can look egotistical. However, your presentation banner outside of the room should introduce you, your topic of the day and show your image. That way your audience will know they're in the right place.

- **Your book:** If you have a book that showcases the thought leadership in your presentation, this can be excellent collateral to reference or even to gift to participants at your workshop or presentation. Just be sure that it relates to the subject matter of your presentation, or it could be perceived as hard selling.

Why does collateral matter?

Collateral is a powerful visual tool for any presentation, speech or keynote. Having visual tools in your presentation looks professional and elevates your entire message, taking it from ho-hum to a place where it can become exceptional.

Of course, visual aids do more than just look good. Having a visual aid helps to:

- Improve the audience's understanding of the content[39]
- Improve the audience's memory of the message[40]

---

39 Bobek, E & Tversky, B. (7 December 2016). 'Creating visual explanations improves learning.' *Cognitive Research: Principles and Implications*. Available at https://doi.org/10.1186/s41235-016-0031-6; Shabiralyani, G, et al. (2015). 'Impact of Visual Aids in Enhancing the Learning Process Case Research: District Dera Ghazi Khan'. *Journal of Education and Practice*. Available at https://files.eric.ed.gov/fulltext/EJ1079541.pdf.

40 Vanichvasin, P. (5 December 2020). 'Effects of Visual Communication on Memory Enhancement of Thai Undergraduate Students, Kasetsart University.' *Higher Education Studies*. Available at https://files.eric.ed.gov/fulltext/EJ1288746.pdf.

"In essence, your collateral helps you to deliver an effective, memorable and exceptional presentation, particularly when they line up with all the touchpoints that you have in your message.

- Provide clear organisation for the content delivery
- Guide the delivery of the speaker
- Aid the memory of the speaker
- Contribute to speaker credibility

In essence, your collateral helps you to deliver an effective, memorable and exceptional presentation, particularly when they line up with all the touchpoints that you have in your message. They engage the audience, provide interest and clarity to your message and help to guide the listener along the path of your presentation.

They also make it easier for you to remember your own content and to deliver it well by providing you with visual reminders of the next point you want to make. Rather than having to memorise your presentation verbatim, you'll have the visual elements to cue your memory and help you to sound natural while delivering your expertise.

At the end of the day, having a speech or presentation that is polished, both verbally and visually, is extremely effective and is part of what will raise you from a good speaker to an exceptional one.

Aligning your visuals with your messaging

Collateral can be very effective in helping to communicate your message, but it's important to make sure the visual experience for your audience matches who you are. This means that all your visual aids, right down to your slides, handouts and even the way you present yourself, must align. Really think about the touchpoints in your message and the visual experience that your audience will engage in. Then consider how you can make this representative of who you are and the message you want to deliver.

A few years ago I flew with Virgin Airlines from Brisbane to Melbourne. They were a client of mine at the time, so I decided to count all the smiles I received from staff from the time I checked in to the time I arrived at my destination. During that time I counted 13 smiles. And those 13 smiles were the key to making me do something – to take action. That action was to return to fly with Virgin again!

This story is a good reminder that it's not just about providing the service of the flight. It's also about the context of the flights and the surrounding experience – the overall visuals. And it's the same for your presentation.

Your slides

Your slides are one of the most important parts of your presentation – whether you're delivering to your internal team or to 500 people. When done well, they can enhance your presentations to no end. But when they're not done well, they can confuse and distract your audience instead.

I once attended a workshop where the entire presentation was written on the slides verbatim. The presenter spent the whole time reading from the slides. Of course, there are more problems here than just the slides – but having all the content on the slides for people to read just meant they checked out from the presentation overall. It was too much information. (And it was much too boring!)

I've also attended presentations where the slides are just stuffed with complex diagrams that would require a PhD to decipher! This approach is not very effective and it left the audience feeling disempowered and disengaged.

So how can you create effective slides to back up exceptional presentations?

1. Use high-quality images and graphics

Ensure that all of the images you use in your presentations are of the highest quality. If you catch yourself saying things like, 'I know this is a bit blurry, but...,' or 'I hope you can see this, but...,' then you have a problem. High-quality images and graphics help your audience to focus on the important elements of your message, rather than being distracted by poor-quality visual images.

The quality of your slides also impacts your personal and professional brand. You don't want to be known as the low-quality presenter.

2. Create a balanced design

Use contrast, alignment, white space and other elements to create a balanced overall design for your slides. This looks good, of course, but more importantly, it helps your audience to focus on the most important elements of your slides and therefore your message. You don't want to use too many fonts, colours or effects that are hard to read, confusing or distracting. You want to make sure the design is simple with elements and content that are relevant and straight to the point.

If you're struggling with this, a good graphic designer can make all the difference.

3. Simple is better

The content included in your slides is also very important. Research has confirmed that people have a limited capacity as to what they can absorb at any given time,[41] so it's important that you have images of what you *want* them to do, not what you *don't* want them to do. After the capacity is reached, the ability of any one person to cognitively grasp any more information is extremely low.

Don't try to cram too much text or information onto the slides – this can make them look boring and unreadable and push people toward their cognitive limit before you've even reached your key messages. Instead, keep it short and simple. Use your slides to highlight the key points in your message using bullet points or keywords.

Nancy Duarte, in her book, *HBR Guide to Persuasive Presentations*, gives great guidelines on how to prepare slides for a presentation:

- Have one clear point on each slide with no more than six lines of text and six words per line. This ensures you keep your message simple and on point.
- If you are including graphs, limit it to one graph per slide. Don't include whole dashboards.
- Use annotations and highlighting, and use sequencing of information as you say it.
- If you are including bullet points, make sure there are no more than three or four bullet points at a time.

---

41 Cowan, N. (1 February 2010). 'The Magical Mystery Four: How is Working Memory Capacity Limited, and Why?' *Current Directions in Psychological Science*. Available at https://www.ncbi.nlm.nih.gov/pmc/articles/PMC2864034/.

"The rule of three
is the principle that
suggests that people
understand concepts and
ideas better when they
are grouped together
in three.

- Use animations so that the content comes up at the same time as you are saying it.[42]

4. *Follow the rule of 3*

The rule of three is the principle that suggests that people understand concepts and ideas better when they are grouped together in three. It's also one of the most effective ways to structure your presentation and so your slides as well.

To use the rule of three, you should limit your slides to three main points and use three supporting elements for each main point. This keeps your message on point and clear, and also helps you to keep your audience from becoming overwhelmed or confused by too much information.

Your handouts

Handouts can be a helpful part of your overall presentation. Importantly, handouts allow your audience to focus more on your speech because they aren't stuck taking notes. And sometimes it will be more practical to include some of your presentation information on a handout, rather than trying to cram all of your points onto the screen.

Many of the same rules apply to your handouts as with your slides, including making sure your handouts are of a good quality and have an attractive layout, colours and typefaces. They should also be fairly simple, jargon free and easy to understand.

But your handouts should also include:

---

42 Duarte, N. (2012). *HBR Guide to Persuasive Presentations (HBR Guide Series)*. Harvard Business Review Press.

- **The key points of your presentation.** Your presentation handout should simply lay out the key points from your speech (this will likely be the three main points and the three supporting points of each main point). Don't rewrite your speech. Just help your audience by giving them the shorthand version so they don't have to take notes themselves.

- **Sources.** If you've referenced other sources, list them in your handout. These might be books or articles for further reading or citations that back up your own research. Providing these to your audience allows you to build authority.

- **Contact information.** Be sure to include your contact information so that the listener can get in touch with you later if they like. You should include your name, job title, website, email and phone number. Make it easy for them to reach out and they'll be far more likely to do so in the future.

Your visual aids should elevate your presentation

As one of my mentors, Keith Abraham, says, make sure your collateral makes you look 10 times better than what you really are! In other words, your visual aids should be helping to elevate you to the level of exceptional. Use each piece of collateral to pull you up higher. If you can do that, then you're going to really have impact in your presentation.

Personal presentation

The last element I want to cover is your personal presentation. This might not generally be considered collateral, but how you look and present yourself to your audience is part of the overall visual elements of your presentation or speech, and in that way it's certainly part of your collateral.

There are some key things to keep in mind when preparing yourself for your presentation.

1. First, dress professionally in an outfit that's easy to look at. For example, try to minimise lots of patterns or different colours on your clothes. If your slides already contain lots of colours and information, then you may wish to choose an outfit in one of those colours or keep your clothing neutral, such as black or navy, so you don't clash with the colours on the screen.

2. Second, understand that your attire is an extension of your personal brand. In my case, I am well known for wearing bright bold colours, and so I try to stick with that theme when presenting. You might be known for wearing neutrals or all black. Staying within your personal brand isn't just a nice-to-have – it's a strong strategy to help people relate to you and remember you.

3. Third, consider your audience and the industry that you're presenting to. If you're delivering a keynote speech to a group of creatives, your style of dress may be different than if you're giving a presentation to small business owners in regional areas. You want to ensure that you dress in a way that makes your audience feel comfortable.

4. Fourth, consider how you will be mic'd. While this is less of a consideration for men, for ladies it might be more practical to wear a skirt or pants and a top when you are presenting so that you can easily slip the microphone up under your shirt. Or if you are wearing a dress, make sure you include a belt which will allow you to do the same. This will make it more likely you

will be able to keep your hands free, instead of having to hold a microphone throughout your presentation.

5. Fifth, both men and women need to think about their hair. It's important that you keep your hair off your face so that it's easier for the audience to see and read your facial expressions. This is extremely important to help them to connect with you. You also want to ensure that you don't have a hairstyle that you'll be fiddling with throughout the presentation, which can be distracting for both you and your audience.

Beyond the stage

Exceptional speakers understand that your physical and digital collateral needs to go beyond the stage. These materials support your expertise, but they also need to provide value and support to the organiser and the audience both before and after your presentation.

Most of the materials will be the same as those we've spoken about above. But how and when you use them matters. Before your presentation or keynote, your focus will be on your bio, headshots, promo videos and intro (for example). These pieces will help generate interest and build credibility before you even take a single step onto the stage.

After you get off the stage, you might want to have a handout or piece of merch with a QR code, a quiz or diagnostic. These allow you to follow up with your audience and have a way to move them from the room to your own database. If you have a book, selling them at the back of the room or even gifting them to participants is a great way to extend your reach and make your presentation more memorable. Your collateral can help you create opportunities long after the applause has faded.

"

Exceptional
speakers understand
that your physical and
digital collateral needs
to go beyond the stage.
These materials support
your expertise.

"

Conclusion

When I think about impact, I think of a lady called Dame Anita Roddick, who opened the doors to The Body Shop in Brighton, England, back in 1976. Her goal was to use business as a force for good by creating ethically sourced and naturally based products in refillable packaging. Over the next four decades, Anita campaigned for many causes, from anti-animal testing to fair trade partnerships. She was a woman who combined profit and purpose and used her voice to make a true impact in the world.

Anita was fond of repeating the Dalai Lama's quote, 'If you think you're too small to have an impact, try going to bed with a mosquito in the room.'

Your slides, your logo, the way you dress – these might all seem like small things. But your collaterals are a vital part of your overall ability to deliver an exceptional presentation, speech, workshop or keynote. They help you take your impact and really amplify it.

Of course, if you want to have true impact in your presentations, then you must ensure that you know your message really well. You need to know your message, connect with stories and analogies and ensure your visual collaterals reflect your message. I think if you can do all of those things, then you're on track to becoming an exceptional speaker and to having great success in all your presentations.

We can all have an impact – and when we use our collaterals to their best advantage – we can have exceptional impact.

CHAPTER 6

EXCEPTIONAL COMMERCIALITY – THE BUSINESS OF SPEAKING

'Outcomes are the currency that buyers understand.'

— Lois Creamer

Being an exceptional speaker is about more than what you say on the stage. You have to be able to make a business of it as well. And unfortunately, this is where many speakers fall down.

For aspiring keynote speakers, the allure of the stage often overshadows the reality of the work behind it. They mistakenly believe that they simply have to get the message and the delivery right (in other words, the performance). But if you'll recall, this was almost my downfall at the beginning of my own speaking career when I got known before I was good. I didn't know what I was doing ultimately, either on the stage or beyond the stage. I needed to learn to speak well... but I also needed to be able to run a speaking business well. And that was another vital learning experience.

When it comes to being an exceptional speaker, you have to become exceptional both on and off the stage. You have to be able to run the business well too. Here are the tips from my own experience, as well as insights from other master speakers in the business, including how to:

1. Set your speaking fees
2. Create a global speaker identity through marketing and branding
3. Get your name out there
4. Get leads from the stage
5. Build client relationships
6. Diversify your revenue stream
7. Add value
8. Be easy to work with
9. Be responsive
10. Consider aftercare
11. Focus on continuous skill development
12. Build your business operations
13. Just start speaking

How to set your speaking fees

Understanding how much you should charge for gigs is a huge part of the business of speaking. And the answer is that it will depend on a few different things. To begin with you really need to be aware of where you are in your speaking journey based on your story, your work, your positioning and the results of your achievements. You also need to understand how much value the event is going to provide for both you and the client. Each of these elements will go into understanding how much to charge.

However, all these variables mean that trying to work out what to charge can be a little bit like diving into a choose-your-own-adventure book. There's no hard and fast rule that you can set and forget – for example, a single hourly rate or even a day rate! You can't even set a rule that you won't do anything for free, because that attitude and mindset can often hinder your growth. Sometimes free is actually really good value for your business growth, your positioning and your marketing overall.

Question 1: How skilled am I at helping this audience?

So when it comes to setting your speaking fees for a particular gig, the first step you need to ask yourself is, 'How skilled am I at helping this audience?' As Matt Church has said, 'A speaker's job is to change the room, and the more that a speaker can change the room, the more they can charge.'

"

When it comes to
being an exceptional
speaker, you have to
become exceptional both
on and off the stage.

"

Question 2: How far along am I on my speaking journey?

For example, I'm currently working with two female keynote speakers – one is an expert in customer experience and customer service, and the other one is an AI expert. I've worked with the customer service expert for the last few years, and each year she's written a new book. She also continues to develop her IP. She researches and writes a regular blog. She has great results with clients and she shares these case studies with her audience as well.

When I started working with her, she was just getting started on her speaking journey, and her business revenue at the time was about $250,000 per year. She was spending most of her practice speaking and delivering training – these are her two big moneymaking modes. So these factors led us to set her fee at $3,000 per keynote.

Question 3: How in demand is my topic?

My other client – the AI expert – is a different story. Her main factor is that she's speaking in a time where her topic is THE topic of the year. Because AI is so hot, and she works in this very specific industry, she's also extremely busy and in demand, and booked very heavily. Regardless of the other factors, the more in demand she gets, the higher the fee she can charge.

Question 4: Who is the audience & what is the gig?

Regardless of where you set your fees, there are also times when you may decide to charge less than your full fee or even deliver for free if it's the right audience and the right gig. For example, if your gig would get you in front of a room of your ideal clients, who are looking for your kind of services, this might be worth doing for free. But if you're speaking at a corporate event with a lineup of other speakers, where the audience is brought by their company and may or may not be your ideal client, you'd want to get your full fee for that event.

Speaking fees breakdown

In general, there are typically about five levels of speaking fees.

LEVEL	FEE RANGE	DESCRIPTION
5	$10,000+	Celebrity-level speaker with widespread recognition (e.g., Brené Brown).
4	$8,000 – $10,000	Motivational speaker, often opening or closing conferences as a 'big ticket' item.
3	$5,000 – $8,000	Thought leader with books, compelling stories, and a dedicated following. Can shift an audience but may not have exceptional craftsmanship yet.
2	$2,000 – $5,000	Subject matter expert with experience and the ability to engage an audience though not necessarily transformational.
1	$0 – $1,000	Honorarium fee, often from charities, Rotary Clubs, meetup groups, or networking events. Low pay but may be the right audience.

Level 1: $0 to around $1,000 is like an honorarium-type fee. You might get this from charity organisations (such as a rotary business), meetup

groups, or networking groups. Often these types of gigs won't pay a lot, but they can be the right audience for you.

Level 2: The second group is a fee that's between about $2,000 and $5,000. At this level you are most likely a subject-matter expert, so you do have expertise. You'll also have some work, background and knowledge at your fingertips, and you'll now be good at being able to hold an audience. However, you may not necessarily be changing a room.

Level 3: The next level up is a fee of between $5,000 and $8,000. At this level the speaker is typically somebody who is a thought leader and expert in their field. They've written the books, they've got all the stories, they know how to shift an audience, and they have a dedicated following. But they may not necessarily be at the stage of real exceptional craftsmanship.

Level 4: At this level you've become a motivational speaker, and you're starting to move from about $8,000 to $10,000 per gig. The 'motivational speaker' will typically be the one to open or close a conference because at this level they've become the big-ticket item.

Level 5: At the highest level, you have the celebrity-type speaker fees. These are typically at $10,000 plus per speaking gig. Put simply, you need to have celebrity-level status to garner these fees. These would be the Brené Browns, for example.

Raising your speaking level & speaker fees

When you're considering what to charge or even raising your fee level, look first at the work that you've done. This is your body of work, as well as your stories, experience and positioning. The next step is then to create your global speaker identity with all the related collateral. The more that you can show clients the value of your messaging and positioning, the more they'll understand how to buy you.

Create a global speaker identity – marketing & branding

We've talked about your speaking brand, how you convey yourself on the stage. But your speaking brand has to be delivered at every touchpoint, not just on the stage. This is how you position yourself in the market and command global-level speaker fees.

If you want to succeed you have to set yourself apart from the vast sea of individuals competing to speak at the same events. You need to define what you want to be known for, find your niche and create your signature brand. There are many ways you can do this, but one of the best is to create a world-class speaker reel.

Speaker reels

Your speaker reel is the first step to differentiate yourself from other speakers, and set up your speaking business for success. Your speaker reel is a visual showcase that demonstrates your core message, shows off your stage presence and lets organisers see the value you offer on the stage itself.

When you're creating your reel, you'll want to show off everything you can do – big events, small events, workshops, presentations. You can include some studio footage that perhaps discusses elements of your speaking work that aren't obvious from your organic footage, and of course, be sure to choose footage that are your best highlights.

Your speaking reel will help you establish your position in the market. Once you have this, you'll need to use it strategically within your practice and within the market, and of course it's pivotal when you approach event organisers.

Speaking collateral

Beyond the speaker reels, you have to build the rest of your collateral. We have an entire chapter dedicated to this, including slides, bios and even your introduction, so we don't need to elaborate here. But it's important to understand that this is part of the business of speaking. Just as important (or more so) as creating invoices, networking and actually delivering the speech or presentation.

Your website

A professional website is your digital storefront. This is your first port of call and the place where you can really showcase who you are, your expertise, your value and how you help your audience. Of course your website needs to house your speaker bio, testimonials, your services and keynotes, a portfolio of past engagements and your speaker reel. It should also make it simple for event organisers to contact you.

In the following chapter, master speaker Deborah Gardner does warn us not to niche too far. Instead, she advises that we should work on creating a single, resource-rich website that caters to your whole audience – clients, event organisers and even speakers bureaus if you

If you want to succeed you have to set yourself apart from the vast sea of individuals competing to speak at the same events.

go that route. You want to be very easy to buy, and your website is one of the best ways to do that.

It's also a great idea to use SEO to optimise your website. This will help that group of people who have a problem you can solve but don't know that you have the answer and help them find you. You should also use LinkedIn, X and other social media platforms to stay visible and connected.

Social proof

Social proof is a great way to show others how you are positioned without having to tell prospective clients yourself. The best way to do this is through referrals (people are always the best social proof and research shows that 88% of people most trust recommendations from people they know[43]). The next great way to do this is to gather and showcase client testimonials. Video feedback is great too (everyone loves video). Case studies and highlighting your work with clients or at events are also great ways to provide social proof and your position in the market.

Get your name out there – speaker bureaus or on your own

There are essentially two primary ways that you can get your name out there as a speaker – either by developing direct relationships with clients or by working with speaker bureaus. In the following chapter,

---

43 (2021). Nielsen 2021 Trust in Advertising Study. Nielsen. Accessed at https://www.nielsen.com/wp-content/uploads/sites/2/2021/11/2021-Nielsen-Trust-In-Advertising-Sell-Sheet.pdf.

Keith Abrahams gives us the six 'Ms' in determining whether or not you want to work with a speaker bureau:

1. Make a decision
2. Model approach
3. Master attraction
4. Money
5. Message
6. Memorable

Use these to determine whether you want to go the bureau route or whether you want to work independently, but, as Keith advises, in today's speaker landscape it's best to choose one or the other.

Making this decision can be tricky. You need to first ask yourself why you might work with a bureau versus doing it yourself.

Things to know about working with a speakers bureau

First, bureaus are very commercial. They want to make money, so they've got to make sure that the speakers they have on their books are the speakers that will be able to close sales. So, if you are on a bureau's books, but you're not heavily booked, this will likely not be for you – as the bureau will likely not put you in front of clients. However, for speakers that are booked heavily, they might understand that now is the time to work with one bureau.

The second thing to remember is that if a bureau is booking you or getting work for you, they're in control. While you're waiting on bookings from bureaus, you may be sitting around twiddling your thumbs (unless you have topic of the year, which I did in 2016 and which had me very busy with the bureaus!). Additionally, they typically take a 30% cut of the keynote fee. That means that if the keynote will pay you $10,000, you will only get $7,000, which is a significant portion of the fee.

Finally, if you get a referral from an event, or you have someone come up to you at the gig and ask you to speak at their event, you'll have to refer that work back through to the bureau. If you do take that client and that sale, the bureau will never book you again.

Third, speaker bureaus often act as order takers who rely on SEO and being found on Google search to market all of their speakers. They don't necessarily go out and do any proactive selling or marketing for any of their speakers. However, they will have a much larger database than you will. This will include clients, meeting planners, conference organisers and more. These are people that you might not typically come across or have in your own database.

Fourth, bureaus are very busy. They are often inundated with requests from people who want to become speakers. So in order to get them to pay attention to you, you really need to be able to pitch well as to why they should put you on their books. Make sure you've got plenty of video of you speaking and, if possible, get them to come and watch you speak if they're in a city where you have a gig. Often bureaus like to be able to see for themselves what you have to offer.

Things to know about going out on your own

First, if you're selling your own speaking, then you're in control. This means you can obviously take your full fee, and you can just take any referrals that come your way without worrying about sending the client back through the speaker's bureau. However, you'll also need to do your own marketing and selling. And this means finding your potential clients. You'll need to determine where they hang out, how you're going to get their details and the best way to contact them. Will it be on LinkedIn? Or do you need to go to networking groups?

Second, over the last few years, I've found that a greater percentage of speakers are choosing to deal more directly with clients than going through the bureaus. This is because many clients are finding the right speakers through their own searches – in particular, Google and AI searches. This does mean you have to have focus on your website and on your SEO so that you're easy to find online.

Third, you'll need to get the right team and resources around you. As Steve Jobs said, *'Great things in business are never done by one person. They're done by a team of people.'* So even if you decide to deal with your clients directly, you'll have to think about what resources (including people resources) can help you market yourself to meeting planners and conference organisers.

My philosophy – do as much as you can by yourself

When it comes to making the choice, my philosophy is to do as much as you can by yourself. If you do get a sale through a bureau, then this is a bit of a bonus. But since you don't have any control over what the bureau does, you just have to take what you can get.

If you do decide to work with the bureaus, it pays to remember this advice from Keith Abraham, *'Be bureau friendly, easy to buy and proactive in developing those relationships. Those speakers that have had huge successes on stage – such as Matt Church and Amanda Gore – have been all in. So be all in. And remember that the bureaus won't come to you – you need to go to them and be sure that you stand out and are memorable.'*

It's also vitally important that you give the bureau everything they need to sell you. This of course includes your speaker kit, showreel, landing page, videos and more. And then I would encourage you to have a look at what you are giving the speaker bureau that they could use for their own contact deals so that any referrals will go back through the bureau.

If you decide to get out there independently, you will need to network, develop your list and foster long-term client relationships. How you do this will depend on where your audience is and what they need from you. But in general, you need to be thinking about the value that you deliver and how you deliver it to them. And this must be part of our speaker business.

Create your own speaking events

Something that can hold many speakers back is that they're waiting for meeting planners and conference organisers to book them to speak. Nowadays, and particularly since COVID, it's becoming more and more competitive to get on stages. The meetings industry has changed. Clients are looking for more value for money and the best of the best.

So if you're not exactly the best of the best or you work in a niche industry, then creating your own events can be a great way to speak and grow your business. The benefit of putting on your own event is that it doesn't need to be for a lot of people. You can hire a private dining room at a restaurant or put on a breakfast and invite your ideal clients. This puts you in front of the right people so you can share your message.

Don't sit around waiting for months. Create your own event that you can speak at in a few weeks and start marketing it. I did this for my own events for 10 years, and it was a great way to grow my client base and position myself as a speaker.

Write the right book

One of the most powerful ways to create positioning and get on stages is to write a book that is relevant to your audience. A book on your topic positions you as an authority and helps you to build trust and confidence with your meeting planner or conference organiser. It doesn't need to be a *New York Times* or even an Amazon best seller. It simply needs to be relevant to your audience.

For example, I wrote a book about medical interview skills (and no, I'm not even a doctor!). This book got me on stage at the Junior Doctor Conference every year for eight years and generated over $1 million in revenue for my practice. It resulted in coaching programs, licencing deals, an online course and a large number of other paid resources that helps doctors apply for their chosen speciality and get through the difficult process of interviews. And all from one book!

Books are one of the best pieces of marketing material you can create. You'll be surprised where it can take you!

Getting leads from the stage

Most speakers who are just starting out are simply trying to become great at speaking on stage. They're happy when they start getting that right and even happier when they begin receiving lovely feedback from people in the audience. But speaking well and getting great feedback is not enough, because it's not a very intentional approach to making speaking work commercial. And most speakers aren't thinking about the money that's left on the table in the room.

Instead, you need to have a commercial focus for all your speaking, and that includes recognising that every time you speak, there are likely people in that room that need more help. Even if it's not right now, there will be a time in the future. These people are leads.

The key to getting leads from speaking is getting the audience into your database. Research from Chet Holmes in his book, *The Ultimate Sales Machine*, shows that only about 3% of any B2B audience are ready to buy or ready for help when they see you speak. A further 6-7% are considering buying now, while the other 90% are on the spectrum between not thinking about buying at this time and definitely not interested.[44]

So your job to get leads from the stage is twofold. First, you need to get these audience members on your database. And second, you need to help those who aren't ready to buy build their readiness by nurturing them over time. You do this by providing content, resources and tools over time so that when they do need help, you are the person that they call.

---

44 Holmes, C. (2008). *The Ultimate Sales Machine: Turbocharge Your Business with Relentless Focus on 12 Key Strategies*. Portfolio.

One of the most powerful ways to create positioning and get on stages is to write a book that is relevant to your audience.

I worked with a gentleman, James Anderson, who is an education expert, consultant, author and speaker. Prior to working with me, he was speaking quite often and getting about 30% of the audience onto his database and email list. This isn't a terrible result, but I knew we could do better. And as a result of the resources and tools that I gave him, he started to achieve about 80% of the audience onto his database, which meant a dramatic increase in practice growth *and* his revenue.

Many of the things that I learned about getting leads from the stage, and that I shared with James, I learned from Keith Abraham. The first time I heard Keith speak, I was already speaking regularly, but I wasn't getting many people opting in. When I shared my problem with him, he asked, 'What are you sharing with people to get them to opt in?' I said, 'I've got a whitepaper.' He said, 'That's just not enough. Five is the magic number. Not three, not six, five.'

At the time I was only getting about 30% opt in, just like James. But I implemented Keith's advice and built out my IP and collateral so that I had five things to give away. And suddenly I was getting about 80% of the room onto my database. The five things you choose should be relevant to your work and your speech. But by way of example, they could be your book, a mini booklet or workbook with key insights and exercises, a branded tool or framework, a meaningful object that relates to your topic (like a small compass or puzzle piece) and a QR code card that links to exclusive content for the attendees. The key is to make these items memorable and tied to your message.

Creating five pieces of collateral to give away at his keynotes was the same advice I gave James, and it worked just as well!

If you're speaking and not getting leads from the stage, it's a little bit like going to a buffet and just having a bread roll. There's so much opportunity in that room, and you really want to make the most of it by optimising the leads that you can get out of it.

To do this, there are two key steps:

1. The first is to create the five things that your audience would find useful or valuable. That might be the items I spoke about above, or handouts, checklists or even a curated list of podcasts or interviews that you might have mentioned in the keynote. The idea is to give your audience practical resources and tools that they can then go away and implement.

2. Second, once you've created those five items, you need to then create a slide for the end of your presentation. This last slide should set out what those five items are and the benefit of each. It doesn't have to be very long, and you should only take about five to seven minutes to go through it. You can then ask the audience to either fill out a form on their table or use a QR code so that they can opt in. This then automatically adds them to your database while they receive all the resources that you've offered to them.

When you approach your speaking with a commercial mindset, you can transform your keynotes from just an engaging presentation (even an *incredibly* engaging presentation), to an engaging presentation that's also a lead-generating opportunity!

Build client relationships

Running a speaker business comes down to one main thing – client relationship management. Your clients are the reason you even have a business, after all!

The basics have to be in place. This is having a customer relationship management tool, like Asana or HubSpot which allows you to track leads, manage workflows and follow up with current and potential clients. Then you need processes in place to be sure you're following up.

When it comes to managing your client relationships, follow up is one of the most important things you can do. After every engagement you should send a thank you email, and set up for a debrief so you can find out what went well and what didn't. This is important every time you speak, of course. But it's also important for every engagement that you have with a client, whether one-on-one or in a corporate setting.

Maintaining your relationships with your clients is huge for potential repeat bookings. Research shows that up to 65% of business comes from existing clients and customers.[45]

Diversify your revenue stream

Being a keynote speaker isn't always a very sustainable way to build a practice – particularly in the beginning. Diversifying your revenue stream is the answer to lumpy revenue (common in any practice, but especially with speakers).

Some ways you can diversify your revenue stream are by leveraging your collateral, creating digital content, coaching and corporate training.

---

45 Merchant, T. (25 August 2023). 'Why retention has become the ultimate growth strategy.' Accountants Daily. Accessed at https://www.accountantsdaily.com.au/business/18967-why-retention-has-become-the-ultimate-growth-strategy.

"

Running a
speaker business
comes down to one main
thing – client relationship
management. Your clients
are the reason you even
have a business,
after all!

"

Leveraging your collateral

Use your books, white papers, newsletters, articles and more to create separate streams of income while reinforcing your expertise. A great example of this is writing a book. When you write a book for your practice, you might get some passive revenue stream from selling the book now and into the future. But even better, you have something to give to clients, to build workshops and diagnostics around, to develop an online course and to share your expertise far and wide.

Your book will open doors for you, whether you mail it to prospective clients, bring it to sales meetings or distribute it at your events to add more value. Unlike networking, your book can reach further and achieve more than one-on-one networking, and it's highly referable. It's very easy for someone to say to another person, 'You'd love this – I'll send you her book!'

It also gives you authority and showcases your expertise in a way that supports workshops, diagnostics, training and other revenue streams too.

All your collateral can be used in this way. And it's a great way to create alternate revenue streams.

Creating digital content

Digital content is a powerful tool for diversifying your revenue stream and allows you to vastly expand your influence beyond the stage. Digital products are accessible and scalable so that you can serve a wider audience while reinforcing your expertise.

- **Online courses –** Packaging your thought leadership into structured digital courses that are downloadable can create passive income and allow participants to engage with your material at their own pace and with a lower barrier to entry. Your online courses might range from foundational or practice topics – your big picture ideas, in other words – to advanced classes that are highly niched.

- **Webinars & virtual events –** Live or recorded webinars allow you to engage with your audience in real-time and in a convenient way for them. You can reach further and wider, even globally, without leaving your office. And it makes it easier than ever to position yourself as a thought leader in your field.

- **Subscription models –** Digital content can also include a subscription service that offers ongoing access to exclusive content, such as master speaker Dr Louise Mahler (who we hear from in the following chapter) offers in her Gravitas Masterclasses. It might also include Q&A sessions, weekly catch-ups and whatever else your audience needs and wants. This can provide recurring income and help you build a loyal community around your brand.

- **Podcasting & video content –** Podcasts and video content created for YouTube or shared on your own website are a great way to leverage your thought leadership. These platforms allow you to connect with audiences who may not be ready (or able) to attend live events but are eager to learn and engage with you. It also allows you to reach people who may not know how valuable your message could be for them.

"
Digital content is
a powerful tool for
diversifying your revenue
stream and allows you to
vastly expand your influence
beyond the stage.
"

Coaching

Coaching is a fantastic way to support your speaking business while also supporting your clients. As a thought leader, you have a wealth of knowledge and experience that others can learn and benefit from. And coaching is a great way to help your clients one-on-one or in a small group, where you can really dive deep into their unique challenges and opportunities. Of course, coaching also helps you create additional revenue streams while making a meaningful impact on clients.

Whether you decide to offer one-on-one coaching or work with small groups (or both!), you'll be in a position to focus deeply on each client and deliver customised strategies for their growth while also supporting your own speaking career.

Corporate training

Corporate training is a lucrative way to bring your expertise into the business world. Many, if not most, organisations need to invest in training programs to upskill their employees, particularly in areas like leadership, communication and collaboration. Often corporate training might be in the form of custom workshops, on-site training sessions or even giving a license to work with your own IP.

Licensing your IP is a unique way to support your own speaking career because it creates a scalable revenue stream with minimal ongoing effort. Rather than you having to deliver every piece of content to every business, you provide them with a licence to do the delivery themselves. This frees you up to speak, coach, do more bespoke training and even focus on growing your thought leadership while being supported by a stream of income.

Corporate training not only enhances your income and supports your speaking but also raises your profile in professional circles, leading to new opportunities.

Add value

When it comes to booking events, we've learned that it's vital that you add value if you want to be memorable, referable, bookable and competitive.

Today's speakers can no longer just deliver – they have to be part of the larger event ecosystem. Event organisers and HR managers in the corporate industry are under immense pressure to fill rooms while finding the right (and interesting!) training and events for their teams.

So one of the best ways to build your success as a speaker is to make their lives easier. And one of the best ways to do this is by adding value that can help them achieve these goals. Providing extra content – like videos, books, diagnostics, blogs, images and more – that can be used in marketing campaigns, as well as helping to promote the event, is an excellent way to add value. You also need to be easy to work with (see the next item!).

Be easy to work with

The days of making extravagant demands are over. Today you need to be visible, available and easy to work with!

Event organisers are looking for speakers who not only deliver incredibly well on stage and have the content that they're looking for, but are also a pleasure to work with behind the scenes. This includes being responsive, flexible and proactive.

You need a reputation for being easy to work with, and then you need to back that up with your actions. One of the best ways to do this is to be responsive (and that's our next tip!). When you have a reputation (and build that with each event you book) for being easy to work with, you become the go-to choice for both repeat bookings and referrals. On the other hand, if it's a challenge to get you on the phone or you make difficult demands, no one will refer you on. That's just the business of speaking!

Be responsive

As we've heard from our master speakers, and as I've seen in my own experience, those who are quickest off the block are the most likely to book gigs. This isn't just because you're 'first in line' so to speak (though that helps in some cases). It's also because those organisers value your responsiveness and it shows that you will be easy to work with.

Event organisers are often juggling tight deadlines and multiple responsibilities. When they reach out, a swift and professional response can make their lives easier *and* set you apart from your competitors.

Always:

- **Prioritise timely communication.** Respond to enquiries, emails and calls as quickly as possible – ideally the same day if possible. Use your team to help you manage this if you need to, particularly if you're travelling or unavailable. They can let the organisers know when they can expect to hear from you.

> The days of making extravagant demands are over. Today you need to be visible, available and easy to work with!

- **Be solutions-oriented.** If someone requests adjustments to your schedule or content, or asks you to tailor part of your delivery or logistics to their event, try to approach these requests with an open mind. If you can be flexible, then do so. When you show that you're willing to accommodate their needs, you can build trust and rapport.

- **Use clear proposals.** When you submit a proposal to an event organiser, make sure it is clear, concise, visually appealing and, most importantly, tailored to the event. Nothing screams 'phoning it in' more than a generic speaker proposal. Also be sure to include your fees, the services you provide, the value-adds you offer and a clear value proposition. This makes it easy for them to say yes to you and to onsell you as well.

Consider aftercare

Don't forget the aftercare. Your relationship doesn't end when you step off the stage (at least it really shouldn't!). If you want to get more opportunities with that client, and be referable to others, you always need to think beyond the stage.

Whenever you book a gig, ask yourself, 'How can I continue to serve this client once the event is over?'

Here are some ways that I suggest:

1. **Thank yous.** Always send a personalised thank you after the event. Depending on the client this may only be an email – or it may be flowers and a hand-written note (this is always my preference). Whatever you do, you need to express your gratitude for the opportunity.

2. **Follow-ups.** It's important that you always follow up with any relevant materials, such as slides, recordings, resources, books and results from the diagnostic from the event.

3. **Request feedback.** Ask for feedback from your event. This not only gives you insight into what you did well and how you can improve in the future, but it also shows that you value their input and are committed to improving.

4. **Explore future opportunities.** Keep the conversation going. Ask if there are other events or teams within their organisation that might benefit from working with you. You can suggest follow-up workshops, additional coaching sessions or tailored resources to meet their needs.

5. **Book a debrief.** Debriefs are a vital part of the business of speaking, and you should book these *at the same time as the event itself.* If it's in the books, it's less likely to be forgotten! A debrief is the perfect time to provide follow-ups in person and give you an opportunity to discuss them. It's also the perfect time to discuss any feedback, giving you a chance to gently suggest exploring future opportunities in a way that's natural and feels like you're offering them solutions rather than looking for sales.

6. **Stay connected.** Add the client to your CRM system and work with your team to maintain regular touchpoints. You can send them updates about your new keynotes, send them any new publications or resources and maintain a personal touch in their lives. This keeps you top of mind when anyone asks, 'Do you know someone...?' and also when they have another event that you might be a good fit for.

Remember that aftercare isn't just about wrapping things up. It's about building lasting relationships that turn one-time clients into long-term partners.

Focus on continuous skill development

As a thought leader, you're only sellable as long as you're relevant. And you can only remain relevant as long as you are continuously developing your skills and expertise. So, to keep your business of speaking going, you also need to keep learning, studying and growing.

How can you do this? You might attend workshops, conferences or courses to refine your speaking *and* business skills. You might follow other experts, study new but complementary fields or invest in your own research. All of these things allow you to stay current and at the forefront of your industry (which is where thought leaders need to be).

Another way to continually develop your skills and expertise is to actively seek (and then incorporate) feedback from audiences and clients as part of your aftercare. Too often we deliver our services, send our thank you notes and then move on to the next client engagement. But client feedback is invaluable to knowing where we can improve. This must be part of our speaking business if we want to stay relevant and sellable, so ensure you have processes in place to seek out this feedback for each and every client engagement.

Build your business operations

When you're a keynote speaker, you have to manage the business operations just like you would for any business. Always use written contracts with clear terms for deliverables, timelines, fees, cancellation policies and usage rights for recordings or materials. You'll want to set up all the systems you need, like Xero or Quickbooks or some other bookkeeping and invoicing software.

You'll also want to consider your legal and insurance needs. Protect your intellectual property, like presentations and branded materials, and always consider whether you need public liability insurance for speaking events.

If you have employees or staff, you'll need to determine pay rates, super payments and the like and arrange all those either yourself or with your book-keeper.

Event preparation

Part of your business preparations has to be event preparation. We've already discussed how exceptional speakers prepare to be on stage. But a lot more goes to delivering at an event.

Work with event organisers to ensure all the technical requirements are correct and to spec. You'll need an audiovisual setup to match your needs, and be sure to have a backup plan for any tech issues. This might be extra adapters or slides on a USB.

You'll also need to have travel and logistics arrangements in place – and you'll need those processes in place in your business so they

"

As a thought leader, you're only sellable as long as you're relevant. And you can only remain relevant as long as you are continuously developing your skills and expertise.

"

happen smoothly and easily for every event and client engagement you undertake. Be sure to include travel costs in your fee.

There may also be event gifts or collateral to be prepared. You may need to have boxes of books printed and ready to distribute. And you'll need to have feedback meetings already scheduled.

In fact, I have a checklist for speaking events for thought leaders that includes 77 tasks and covers everything from the first step of having your team book time with you to set up the project, through to creating a run sheet and even booking parking if needed. All of these little steps matter and make the process smooth for you and for the event organiser.

All of this is the business of speaking. And it takes planning and processes that need to be built into the structure of your business to go well.

Just start speaking

The final step in the business of speaking is to just start speaking. No matter how small the gig is, just get going. I did about a hundred free gigs before I got paid, and that meant that I got a lot of exposure and a lot of contact details for my list because I got a lot of people seeing me speak. And if you're a great speaker, you'll soon find your way onto bigger stages and into bigger, and higher-paying gigs!

Conclusion

The business of speaking is about more than just delivering exceptional content from the stage. It's about building a sustainable, professional business that reflects your value, expertise and, most importantly, commitment to serving clients. When you focus on your brand, your client relationships, your processes and continually improving your skills and thought leadership, you can create a thriving speaking career that leaves a lasting impact – for you and your clients.

Remember, the most successful speakers don't just inspire their audiences – they've also mastered the art of running their business. And they do both with passion and care!

CHAPTER 7

INSIGHTS FROM MASTER SPEAKERS

*'The only reason to give a speech
is to change the world.'*
— **President John F. Kennedy**

Every exceptional speaker has a spark that sets them apart. A commitment to changing minds. A desire to stir emotions. And an ability to inspire action. Behind the polished delivery and memorable sound bites lies a blend of passion, preparation and persistence that elevates them to a level beyond the norm. Master speakers don't just share information. They transform audiences.

In this chapter we'll explore the journeys and approaches of four of these master speakers – Keith Abraham, Dr Louise Mahler, Deborah Gardner, Sally Foley-Lewis and Lois Creamer. We'll see how each has mastered the art of connecting with audiences in distinct and powerful ways and glean insights from their experiences about what makes a speaker truly remarkable.

Keith Abraham – The Godfather of Speaking in Australia

If you're on the speaking circuit, you'll certainly have heard the name Keith Abraham. In fact, he's almost synonymous with keynote speaking and has been at the forefront of the professional speaking industry here in Australia and globally for over 20 years. He has spoken to audiences in 23 countries and worked with over 300 companies. And across his time as a speaker, he's become well known for his ability to inspire, engage and even transform his audiences.

But of course, it didn't happen overnight.

Keith has committed the past two decades to understanding how high-performing experts and thought leaders can achieve their goals of being expert keynote speakers. His extensive research has shown him that the best way to truly change an audience is to create a connection between your personal passion and your professional performance. And his goal is to help people harness their passion, achieve their goals and focus on what's most important to bring the best out of themselves and their business. He establishes a true goal alignment and enables individuals to live their personal and professional lives, energised and with focused direction.

And this has led to incredible success. Keith has received the Speaker of the Year Award from the Professional Speakers Association, Educator of the Year and the Nevin Award, the highest honour for professional speaking. And he has been ranked the 'Best Keynote Speaker' at more than 2,870 conferences over the last 28 years.

Despite his success, Keith remains incredibly humble and grounded. His colleagues and others in the speakers circuit affectionately refer to him as the 'Godfather' of speaking in Australia.

I remember the first time I met Keith at Professional Speakers Australia (known as PSA). It was one of the first programs I had attended, and at the time I was writing LinkedIn profiles for people. When we met, I asked him if I could please write his LinkedIn profile. And he let me! This is how we got to know each other, and then we went on to be in a mastermind together for over seven years. He has also been a huge supporter of me and our Women with Influence programme. And not just with me – he's known as being Mr Generosity because he's always trying to help people become the best in their field.

His influence extends far beyond his own work, as he has mentored and inspired many aspiring speakers. His generous nature and willingness to share his knowledge have cemented his status as a trusted figure in the speaking community. And today he shares his insights to educate other speakers through his books and online courses.

🔑 Key insights from Keith on exceptional speaking

During a recent conversation at our Elevate Day, Keith Abraham shared valuable insights into the world of keynote speaking. He believes that it's important to be focusing on the evolving relationship between speakers and speaker bureaus, and how we can connect, collaborate and capitalise on those bureau relationships. He also shares some general insights on how to become an exceptional speaker too.

Speaker bureaus

When considering how (or whether) to work with speaker bureaus, Keith says there are six 'Ms' that we should consider.

1. **Make a decision.** 25 years ago you could kind of do both – work with bureaus or get your own clients. Today he thinks that the best way forward is to make a decision of one or the other. And if you decide to work with bureaus, be bureau-friendly, easy to buy and proactive in developing those relationships. Those speakers that have had huge successes on stage – such as Matt Church and Amanda Gore – have been all in. So be all in. And remember that the bureaus won't come to you – you need to go to them, and be sure that you stand out and are memorable.

2. **Decide your model.** If you're going to engage with the speakers bureaus, decide what model approach you will take. Will you look at an exclusive relationship, an agency relationship or perhaps two-prong marketing?

3. **Attract, convert, deliver.** If you're going to get on stages, you have to master three things – attract, convert, deliver. The speakers who have got full schedules and command high fees are exceptionally good at attracting enquiries, converting these to paying gigs and then delivering with incredible competency.

4. **Money.** When it comes to your fee, think about what you can charge that feels right. Then consider how you can offer more value (upsell) and how you can become better at what you do. Then think how you might be more referable and generate more business.

5. **Message.** Ask yourself, what do you want to be famous for? And what do you want to be known for in your presentations? You need to really nail this down in order to become the exceptional speaker you want to be.

6. **Memorable.** Ask yourself, how do you become memorable? The key here is becoming memorable with your clients and the bureaus you work with. You do this by building your list of people with whom you want to build a relationship. Contact them and meet them.

General insights

1. **Get the right support.** If you're struggling to move forward, ask yourself, what challenge is slowing you down from achieving your goals? Then find the right person to help you overcome that challenge.

2. **Don't give up.** With your clients, it can sometimes be a long, slow burn before you get on their stage. Just keep at it.

3. **Keep marketing.** Don't stop marketing, even if you get busy! If you want to maintain your speaking business, contact seven people a week. If you want it to grow, contact seven people a day. And if you want hyper growth contact 14 people a day.

4. **Practise!** To create a killer keynote you must practise and refine it. You should deliver it to various audiences – even free – and this will help you master your delivery, storytelling and stage presence.

5. **Learn from your mistakes.** When you are preparing to be an exceptional speaker, mistakes are not failures, they're learnings.

Keith Abraham's influence on the speaking industry is undeniable. Through his relentless dedication to helping others, his complete dedication to the craft of speaking, and his focus on aligning personal passions and professional goals, he has created a lasting legacy that goes beyond just his impact on audiences. He has shown the speaking world that exceptional speaking isn't just about being on stage – it's about being remembered, trusted, respected and, most importantly, connecting and inspiring others.

Dr Louise Mahler – Leadership, Body Language & the Power of Voice

Dr Louise Mahler is a renowned expert in the fields of leadership communication, body language and voice, and I'm privileged to have been able to work closely with her and to have learned so much about exceptional speaking from her. Because for Louise, it's not just about the content of the message – but so much about the delivery.

Louise has a unique blend of business acumen, having an economics degree in statistics, and performance skills, having spent years on international stages pursuing her other passion – opera singing. But it was after leaving her performance life and returning to the corporate world that she found what has been the driving force behind her practice – helping others to understand and use body language for exceptional speaking. She describes this as a 'calling rather than a profession'. Louise says, 'If I didn't get paid, I'd do it for free.' That's how important it is for her!

Louise teaches her clients and community about how to communicate with gravitas (that is, with the power of trust and influence), utilising a deep understanding of how both the body and voice impact leadership and influence. And this has led her to become one of the most sought-after keynote speakers and leadership coaches in Australia.

Her expertise spans speaking, coaching, retreats and media analysis, where she brings her deep knowledge of body language and vocal dynamics to life. Her clients span industries, and her work is centred on helping professionals – from corporate executives to aspiring leaders – develop their confidence, credibility and presence on stage and in the boardroom. She is also a regular contributor to print, radio and television media and is a regular on Channel 7.

Louise is also an author, sharing her wisdom and insights in her most recent book, *Gravitas: Timeless Skills to Communicate with Confidence and Build Trust*. She discusses how ancient virtues and understanding can help leaders transform their presence and impact as a leader today.

When it comes to her keynote speaking, Louise is known for her high-energy, transformative presentations that leave audiences inspired and ready to take action. She is particularly good at engaging with her audiences with humour and then holding their attention despite presenting distinctive and sometimes challenging ideas. And her innovative approach to voice and leadership (and translating this for presentations and keynotes) has earned her incredible accolades, including being recognised as a Top 30 Global Guru in body language and communication and earning the coveted 2021 Keynote Speaker of the Year with PSA.

With all this experience, what are Louise's key insights on elevating speaking to exceptional speaking?

🔑 Key insights from Dr Louise Mahler on exceptional speaking

During a recent podcast episode, Dr. Louise Mahler shared the philosophies that guide her work and how she thinks leaders should be looking to elevate their communication today, including on stages and in presentations. And not surprisingly, this was often around the idea of body language and delivery!

1. **Voice and body matter.** Louise believes that we often block our communications, particularly on stage, by the way we use our voice and bodies. For example, tension in your jaw comes out in your voice and can create an impression of anger or aggression. And the way you stand impacts your ability to freely breathe, which can strangle your voice and impact your credibility and trust. By releasing these

physical blockages you can transform your voice and body language, leading to better health outcomes and improved communication.

2. **Confidence and credibility.** When you have more control over your body and voice, you'll find your self-confidence is significantly improved. And that in turn can significantly improve your influence on your audience. 'You will lose trust if you're holding your breath,' Louise says. When people break their sound or hold tension in their voice, it undermines their credibility and ability to influence others.

3. **A framework for excellence.** Louise has created a model that helps leaders visualise their progression from initial performance levels to mastery – the aim is to help clients consistently perform at an exceptional level regardless of the circumstances. Following a framework minimises your prep time for presentations.

4. **Learning what we don't know.** Most leaders today haven't been taught the skills that the ancient Greek and Roman orators knew – and today's training, often centred around speech pathology or acting skills, simply doesn't address communication needs. 'There are 32 fields of voice, and none adequately address voice for people in business,' Louise explains.

This gap in the literature drove her to develop her own methodologies, grounded in both her personal experience and academic research. Louise believes embracing the skills of body language and delivery bridges this gap and can help leaders who have lost confidence in speaking to regain that mindset of belief in themselves.

5. **Women speakers can have gravitas too.** Too often we've been taught that gravitas belongs to men. That's simply not true. Women have everything they need to communicate and appear on stages to convey trust and build impact with their audiences.

For Louise, speaking is about creating a lasting impact, and she takes pride in knowing that her work continues to resonate with audiences long after the event has ended. Her holistic approach, focusing on both perception and health, sets Louise apart from traditional communication and speaking coaches and elevates her to a true master speaker.

Deborah Gardner – From Olympic Trials to the Meetings Industry & Speaking Success

Deborah Gardner is a highly respected professional speaker, hotel sales veteran and a certified meeting professional. But one of the things that sets Deborah apart is the fact that she came into her new practice from a life in sports. In fact, she was not only a competitive Olympic Trials swimmer, but she was also the first female broadcaster with CBS Sports. This background helped to set her up to become a leading voice in the meetings and hospitality industry. But it's in her speaking on stages that Deborah found her calling.

I saw Deborah speak in her hometown of Phoenix, Arizona in July 2016. And I was literally blown away. Her presentation was practical, useful and incredibly insightful. In fact, even though it was a five-day conference, and Deborah spoke on the first day, I could have hopped on a plane after day one completely content that I had gotten the value I needed from the conference – she was that good.

Deborah's speciality and platform is 'Don't Quit, Do It', and this mirrors what she is known for in her industry. But it also resonates with a much wider audience, which is why she's been asked to present at hundreds of hospitality industry organisations throughout North America. She has also been recognised as one of only five speakers worldwide to receive the Certified Meeting Professional designation, has been honoured as the Convention Industry Council's Top 30 Most Influential Meeting Professionals and named as *Meeting and Convention Magazine*'s favourite speaker from a poll of their readers.

When it comes to her speaking career, Deborah started off a little shaky. She says, 'As a swimmer in college, I wasn't really allowed to work, but yet on campus I was given an opportunity to be a public address announcer for an activity that was happening on campus. And I look at it as my first speaking engagement in front of 14,000 people.

'But unfortunately I announced the wrong mascot and got booed by 14,000 people. And the ironic thing was, the time that this happened, I realised that they were actually broadcasting this on CBS, which I ironically ended up working for down the road. So it's been kind of an interesting road for me to get where I am today.'

Deborah's work today helps to bridge the gap between decision-makers and speakers while emphasising resilience and success. So what are her key insights when it comes to exceptional speaking?

🔑 Key insights from Deborah Gardner on exceptional speaking

Deborah Gardner's extensive experience in both the hospitality and speaking industries offers valuable insights into not just what it takes to succeed as a speaker but also what it takes to elevate your delivery to become an exceptional speaker.

1. **Adapt to industry changes and challenges.** Like all industries, the speaking industry can be disrupted by pandemics or economics, or many other challenges. These disruptions can significantly impact costs and budgets for businesses looking to hire speakers. If we can understand these challenges, we'll be in a better position to demonstrate our value in a way that resonates with those booking the gigs and that makes us more bookable and referable.

2. **Building relationships is key.** Deborah teaches us how important it is for speaking success to build chemistry with event professionals before even speaking with them. This means having an organised and up-to-date online presence to help those people who are researching you. And it's vital to respond quickly to phone calls and emails, as this can be key to setting you apart from your competition. She says, 'If you're a good speaker that returns phone calls faster than great speakers, you will get the job.'

3. **Add value to your events.** Speakers no longer just deliver – they have to be part of the larger event ecosystem. Meeting professionals today are under immense pressure to fill rooms and sell tickets. So one of the best ways to build your

success as a speaker is to make their lives easier by adding value that can help them achieve these goals. You can do this by providing extra content – such as videos and blogs – that can be used in marketing campaigns, as well as helping to promote the event. The days of making extravagant demands are over. Today you need to be visible, available and easy to work with!

4. **Leverage trends and stay flexible.** Things are always changing in the speaking industry, and we need to respond to those trends and stay flexible if we want to be successful speakers. One example Deborah mentions is the rise of esports and how this $600 million industry is influencing the types of venues that are available for corporate speaking events. This means that we're seeing smaller events being pushed into new and creative spaces such as bowling alleys and museums. Being flexible and adaptable so you can deliver in a wide variety of settings is important and will allow you to embrace new opportunities for speakers, too.

Deborah's practical advice, deep understanding of the industry and commitment to helping others improve their working relationships with meeting professionals make her a standout leader in the world of public speaking and event management. Her tips – stay informed, stay flexible and always be prepared to add value – can help us all become more exceptional speakers.

Sally Foley-Lewis – Mastering the Art of Keynote Speaking with Authenticity & Interaction

Sally Foley-Lewis is a brilliant and award-winning speaker and expert in middle management leadership development. She's known for her genuine and interactive approach to presentations and her work empowering managers and leaders.

Sally began her career as a trainer and facilitator, and, unlike many speakers who confine themselves strictly to the 'keynote label', she continues to work in each of these spaces, integrating her training and facilitation work with her coaching and speaking work. Integrating each of these elements in her presentations gives her a unique point of difference, keeps her audiences engaged and makes her a standout in her field.

Sally's unique approach sets her apart from other, more traditional keynote speakers. Bringing in the interactive elements is key to how she gets her audience to actively engage with her message. She calls this her ability to 'dance' between modes – trainer, speaker, facilitator – and it keeps her sessions dynamic and impactful.

Coming to terms with calling herself a keynote speaker, even as just one of her labels, was something Sally admits she wrestled with. For her, the key challenge was accepting the mindset shift from someone delivering short training sessions to someone inspiring and motivating a wider audience through a keynote. The journey of self-belief took years to settle in, but now she confidently claims her place on the stage.

Sally also has a dedication to continuous improvement. This is evidenced by her investment in extensive coaching and speaker training, which helps her deliver presentations that not only land but also resonate deeply and personally with her audience. Through her keynote speaking, she's able to help upskill managers, boost productivity and help her listeners embrace their own self-leadership. And she does it all with a wicked sense of humour and a speaking style that makes people feel completely at ease!

When I asked her why she thought speaking matters so much in a thought leader's practice, she said, 'It shows your ability to think uniquely or from different angles around something you're an expert in. Being able to speak eloquently and motivationally about it lets the audience see how much of a thought leader you are.' Exactly right!

So what are Sally's top tips on exceptional speaking?

🔑 Key insights from Sally Foley-Lewis on exceptional speaking

1. **Don't wait for paid gigs.** Speaking for free can open doors within organisations that will pay future dividends in your practice. You can speak at webcasts, webinars, association events, networking evenings and even on podcasts. Speaking for free at places like Rotary or Toastmasters can also help when you're just starting.

2. **Speak often and speak everywhere.** Get yourself on stages, often and everywhere. Darren Lacroix, a world champion speaker, emphasised, 'Stage time, stage time, stage time.' If anyone invites you to speak and you say no,

you're doing yourself a disservice. Every opportunity you get, create it and take it.

3. **Do the work.** Sally advises that one big mistake thought leaders and emerging speakers make is thinking that just because they wrote a book, made a website and put up a LinkedIn profile, they'll get speaking gigs. It doesn't work that way. You have to do the work and go get them.

4. **Think about how you're reaching out.** The human connection is vital, and forgetting that is a mistake. If you're reaching out for gigs and not getting replies, it's time to look at *how* you're reaching out. Are you connecting? Are you building relationships? If not, think about how you can change that.

5. **Get started.** If you have a consulting or advisory practice, start building the speaking part of that business now. Start with PSA. They have chapters in almost every state, run online programs and will get you involved with a community of people who also enjoy speaking and can help you with both the craft and business of speaking.

Sally Foley-Lewis exemplifies the art of delivering interactive, impactful presentations that are truly authentic. Her journey highlights the value of utilising your own unique blend of skills, and staying adaptable to really connect with your audience. Rather than shifting *from* trainer and facilitator *to* keynote speaker, Sally evolved into a trainer, facilitator, coach *and* keynote speaker – demonstrating the importance of mindset, perseverance and continuous improvement. And her message is clear – don't just wait for the perfect opportunity – create it!

Lois Creamer – Turning Outcomes into Impact

If you haven't spent time in Lois Creamer's world, you are missing out. Lois is a powerhouse in the world of professional speaking, and she's renowned not just for her speaking ability but also for her ability to help other speakers thrive in the speaking business. Her expertise lies in her ability to help speakers find their true value so that they move from being performers to valuable resources for their clients.

Lois is based in the US, but she's also well known among Australian-speaking professionals, and she's a key supporter of the PSA community. Her book, *Book More Business*[46], is considered the bible for speakers who are looking to succeed in the highly competitive speaking industry. In the most recent edition she delves into modern challenges like AI integration and the need to be amenable to the short lead times for event bookings.

From Lois we learn that speaking is not just about performing – it's about delivering our IP. She says that most speakers struggle when asked, 'What do you do?' She says, 'They often answer, "I speak on sales," or "I speak on leadership," and I think that's a missed opportunity. Especially now, we deliver our services in multiple ways. We're not just speakers; we're purveyors of intellectual property. Speaking is just one way we bring it to the market. Successful speakers are also consultants, coaches, authors, and more. But it all starts with being able to describe the outcomes you bring.'

---

46 Creamer, L. (1 July 2017). *Book More Business: Make Money Speaking.* Silver Tree Publishing.

Lois teaches us that when we're booking an event, we need to be able to share both our concept and an outcome – not just a topic. Lois says, 'Instead of saying, "I'm a consultant in the speaking industry," I'd say, "I work with speakers, consultants, and experts who want to book more business, make more money, and monetise their message." This turns the conversation from topic to outcomes, and outcomes are really the currency buyers understand.

Lois understands that speaking well is about understanding your value, targeting your niche and understanding (and striving for) your desired outcomes. Because at the end of the day, we can't be exceptional speakers if we can't do well at the actual business of speaking!

Lois insists that exceptional speakers need to focus on what they can offer beyond the stage. They need to be able to create lasting relationships and become indispensable resources for their clients. Her philosophy – 'specialisation builds trust' – builds on the fact that specialisation is the key to breaking into new markets, including the US-speaking market.

Because there's a much greater cost to bringing Australian speakers to the US market (think flights, accommodation and other expenses), you must have an extremely strong value proposition. You will need to be able to show that you 'hold the keys to kingdom' so to speak. In other words, that you have the specific expertise that can be applied to the organisers' market and their needs.

Another way to get an in is to try to work with a larger corporation or association that allows you to do multiple programs while you're in the US (or other area). This can spread out the cost for the organisers and make it more viable.

Many speakers, particularly new speakers, believe that casting a wide net will gain them more interest and more speaking gigs. But Lois' work shows us that actually, being specific and targeting your niche is much more effective.

Finally, Lois' advice is that in the coming year or two, lead times will be shorter, and organisations will hold onto their budget until the very last minute. It's important for speakers to be able to quickly and flexibly respond to requests for speaking gigs.

Lois also talks about the importance of aftercare – that is, what you can offer after an event to continue serving the client. This might be a follow-up workshop or Q&A session. It could be the results from a diagnostic with actionable steps. It could also be a follow-up meeting discussing what did and didn't work well (I always recommend this one regardless). This type of aftercare builds relationships and creates additional revenue streams, turning you from a speaker into a trusted resource, which is the highest calling.

Lois' focus on turning every speaking engagement into a stepping stone for deeper client relationships is certainly the thing that elevated her to master speaker status.

🔑 Key insights from Lois Creamer on exceptional speaking

1. **Craft a strong value proposition.** Don't just describe what you do – articulate the outcomes you deliver.

2. **Specialisation builds trust.** Generalists will always struggle to stand out. But when you target a specific niche and show

how you're an expert in that space, you'll attract the right opportunities.

3. **Don't forget the aftercare.** Always think beyond the stage. Ask yourself, 'How can I continue to serve this client?'

4. **Adapt to market changes.** The speaking industry is evolving rapidly. Be willing and open to change.

5. **Invest in long-term relationships.** No matter how you book your speaking gigs, focus on building a relationship with those organisers. Respond quickly, stay organised and always aim to make life easier for decision makers.

Looking to Master Speakers

Keith Abraham, Louise Mahler, Deborah Gardner, Sally Foley-Lewis and Lois Creamer are all incredible examples of exceptional speakers and their insights highlight the diverse paths and philosophies that can each lead to incredible success on stages. They show us that there's no one-size-fits-all formula. But a few universal themes emerge, which I hope we've also highlighted throughout this book – dedication to your craft, the courage to be authentic and the relentless drive to connect with your audience.

However, if you truly want to be an exceptional speaker, don't stop with Keith, Louise, Deborah, Sally or Lois. Find the master speakers that you admire, study them, learn from them, even ask them to mentor you. It's this drive to improve and learn from those who are masters of their craft that will see you changing the world, one speech at a time.

IN CLOSING

Remember the Jerry Seinfeld quote in Chapter 1?

'According to most studies, people's number one fear is public speaking. Number two is death. Death is number two. Does that sound right? This means to the average person, if you go to a funeral, you're better off in the casket than doing the eulogy.'

My sincere hope is that you now know you don't have to be a natural speaker to be world-class or to be able to grow your practice and your revenue from your speaking ventures. My other hope is that this book has helped you to go from feelings of fear and inadequacy (and we've all felt them!) to feelings of strength and capability when you face public speaking. And that you'd rather choose the eulogy over the casket!

Remember that the key to exceptional speaking that leads to impactful presentations is exceptional content, exceptional connection, exceptional collateral and exceptional commerciality. So, you need to know your content, you need to connect with your audience, you need to create strong, aligned collateral and you need to do it with a commercial approach. If you can do that – following the steps and suggestions in this book – then you will truly attain 'Rockstar' status.

I know you can do it!

IT'S TIME TO START THE CONVERSATION

The concepts, suggestions and steps in this book are designed to start the conversation, to inspire you and to lead you along the path to becoming a better, more confident, and absolutely exceptional speaker. Your job is now to take these concepts and apply them to yourself so that you can build connection, trust and influence in your audience and all those who come in contact with your brand.

These concepts build the framework for you to see where you already have strengths in place (perhaps knowing your content is a strength) and where there may be areas of improvement (perhaps you need stronger collateral). As you improve each area, you'll begin to see your speaking confidence and capabilities soar until you're easily creating and presenting with real impact.

Don't be afraid to take small steps. You don't have to do everything at once. But taking steps to begin to create more impact in your presentations will lead to a process of continuous levelling up that will soon see you achieving your goals.

I would love to hear how you go implementing these concepts and strategies and the outcomes you see in your own speaking confidence, capabilities and, ultimately, impact. Please get in touch with me at jane@jane-anderson.com.au to share.

I'm cheering you on!

Jane

WORK WITH JANE

In a world of constant change, there is a greater need for consultants and experts in their fields to lead and help their clients navigate change. To do this they need a highly influential personal brand, catalyst content and effective business support.

With over 25 years' experience and named as one of the top three branding experts in the world, Jane has helped over 200,000 people to build their identity and influence. She is a certified speaker, coach and has been featured on *Sky Business*, *The Today Show*, *The Age*, *Sydney Morning Herald*, *BBC* and *Management Today*.

The author of 14 books, Jane typically speaks at conferences, runs workshops, consults and coaches. She also has a particular focus on female leaders, helping them to build their personal brands, thought leadership and sales.

Jane holds one of the top 1% viewed LinkedIn profiles and is the host of the *Jane Anderson Show* podcast, where she has interviewed modern thinkers such as Seth Godin.

She has also won over 45 marketing, business and coaching industry awards.

CORPORATE CLIENTS HAVE INCLUDED:

Telstra, International Rice Research Institute, Wesfarmers, Amadeus, Virgin Australia, IKEA, LEGO, Mercedes-Benz Australian Medical Association, Shell Energy and WorkCover.

Book in a time to chat here: https://calendly.com/jane-0877/complimentary-discussion or contact Jane's team at support@jane-anderson.com.au or +61 7 3841 7772.

Alternatively, jump on Jane's website at www.jane-anderson.com.au to find out about her workshops, speaking and coaching programs.

OTHER TITLES

BY JANE ANDERSON

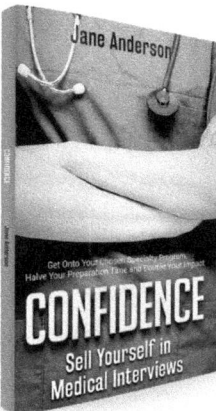

www.ingramcontent.com/pod-product-compliance
Lightning Source LLC
Chambersburg PA
CBHW071602210326
41597CB00019B/3374